AMOS

T. J. Betts

I have known T. J. Betts for a number of years. He was raised in a pastor's home, and he is a pastor/scholar who writes for the local church. Using personal illustrations and practical applications in this commentary, he shows how the writings of an eighth-century B.C. prophet still speak to the 21st century church.

Chuck Lawless
Vice-President for Global Theological Advance,
International Mission Board, Southern Baptist Convention

What a wonderful gift to the pastor who wants to allow the text of Scripture to drive his sermon. T. J. Betts' commentary will be ready at hand when I prepare to teach from the prophet Amos. It is a treasure trove for the serious expositor.

Daniel L. Akin
President, Southeastern Baptist Theological Seminary,
Wake Forest, North Carolina

T. J. Betts comes to the text of Amos with a scholarly mind and a pastoral heart. His judgments about the text are carefully considered and sound, and his prose is warm and direct. Pastors who have found the task of preaching from the prophets daunting will discover in this volume helpful material for historical background, theological interpretation, and homiletical application.

Duane Garrett
John R. Sampey Professor of Old Testament Interpretation,
The Southern Baptist Theological Seminary, Louisville, Kentucky

Books on the Old Testament tend to be either technical and tedious or superficial and moralistic. Once in a while we discover one that breaks the mould. T. J. Betts has done it! He tells us not only what Amos means but also why it matters. He proves again that the expositor's task is not to make the Bible relevant, but to simply show how relevant it is!

Alistair Begg
Senior Pastor, Parkside Church, Chagrin Falls, Ohio

AMOS

An Ordinary Man with
an Extraordinary Message

T. J. Betts

CHRISTIAN FOCUS

T. J. Betts is Associate Professor of Old Testament Interpretation at The Southern Baptist Theological Seminary in Louisville, Kentucky and has been a pastor for over fourteen years and a professor of Old Testament for over ten years. He is also the author of *Ezekiel the Priest: A Custodian of Tôrâ* and has written for The Southern Baptist Journal of Theology and Biblical Illustrator as well as contributed to The Challenge of the Great Commission and the Holman Illustrated Bible Dictionary. He received his B.S.ED. from Wright State University, and his M.Div. and Ph.D. in Old Testament literature from The Southern Baptist Theological Seminary.

Unless otherwise indicated all Scripture quotations are taken from *The Holy Bible, English Standard Version*, copyright © 2001 by Crossway Bibles, a division of Good News Publishers. Used by permission. All rights reserved.

Scripture quotations marked "NASB" are taken from the *New American Standard Bible*®, Copyright © 1960, 1962, 1963, 1968, 1971, 1972, 1973, 1975, 1977, 1995 by The Lockman Foundation. Used by Permission. www.lockman.org

Scripture quotations marked "NIV" are taken from *The Holy Bible, New International Version*®. NIV®. Copyright © 1973, 1978, 1984 by International Bible Society. Used by permission of Zondervan. All rights reserved.

Copyright © T. J. Betts

ISBN 978-1-84550-727-5

10 9 8 7 6 5 4 3 2 1

Published in 2011
in the
Focus on the Bible Commentary Series
by
Christian Focus Publications Ltd.,
Geanies House, Fearn, Ross-shire,
IV20 1TW, Scotland, UK.
www.christianfocus.com

Cover design by Alister MacInnes

Printed and bound by
Bell & Bain, Glasgow

All rights reserved. No part of this publication may be reproduced, stored in a retrieval system, or transmitted, in any form, by any means, electronic, mechanical, photocopying, recording or otherwise without the prior permission of the publisher or a licence permitting restricted copying. In the U.K. such licences are issued by the Copyright Licensing Agency, Saffron House, 6–10 Kirby Street, London, EC1 8TS www.cla.co.uk.

Contents

1. An Unlikely Prophet with an Unsavory Task (Amos 1:1-2) 7
2. Judgment on Israel's Neighbors (Amos 1:3–2:5) 19
3. The Wrong Way to Respond to God's Grace (Amos 2:6-16) 41
4. The Privilege of Responsibility (Amos 3:1-15) 57
5. Expressions of Self-centeredness (Amos 4:1-13) 71
6. Seek God, and Live (Amos 5:1-17) 85
7. Confidence Isn't Everything (Amos 5:18-27) 99
8. The Peril of Complacency (Amos 6:1-7) 113
9. The Fall of the Proud (Amos 6:8-14) 121
10. Judgment, Intercession, and Mercy (Amos 7:1-9) 131
11. Who's the Boss? (Amos 7:10-17) 143
12. The End of a Season (Amos 8:1-14) 153
13. The Judgment of God (Amos 9:1-10) 171
14. The Lord: The One True Promise Keeper (Amos 9:11-15) 181

    Conclusion 193

Subject Index 195
Scripture Index 200

In loving memory of my father
Charles D. Betts
1934-2007
who taught me to love Christ and His Church

I

An Unlikely Prophet with an Unsavory Task

(Amos 1:1-2)

The Book of Amos begins (1) by introducing the prophet for whom the book is named, (2) by telling us something of the times in which his prophetic activities occurred, and (3) by revealing something of the nature of his message.

What may we know of Amos the man?

The book gives us little information concerning Amos' personal life. His name may derive from the Hebrew verb meaning 'to load' or 'to carry a load or burden.' Certainly, Amos had a load to bear as he delivered God's message. One scholar has suggested that the name may have been given to Amos by the recipients of his message who saw the prophet himself as a burden or pain.[1] In other words, they might have said something like, 'Here comes that "Pain" to give us more grief by preaching at us.' If so, Amos seemed to be willing to take on such an epithet if it meant he was being obedient to God's call upon his life. Another possible meaning to Amos' name is 'one sustained by Yahweh.'[2] Certainly, Yahweh did sustain Amos as he faced opposition to his ministry.

---

1. Gary G. Cohen and H. Ronald Vandermey, *Hosea and Amos,* Everyman's Bible Commentary (Chicago: Moody Press, 1981), 86.
2. Johann Jacob Stamm, 'Der Name des Propheten Amos und sein sprachlicher Hintergund,' in *Prophecy: Essays Presented to Georg Fohrer on His Sixty-fifth Birthday, 6 September 1980* (BZAW; ed. J. A. Emerton; New York: Walter de Gruyter, 1980), 137-42.

Furthermore, the text tells us that Amos was 'among the sheepherders of Tekoa' (1:1). Tekoa was about ten to eleven miles south of Jerusalem, five miles south of Bethlehem, and about eighteen miles from the Dead Sea. He lived on the border between two very different types of landscape. To his east was the barren wilderness that stretched to the Dead Sea, and to his west were the fertile agricultural lands of Judah that reached to the coastal plain on the edge of the Mediterranean Sea. He lived in a land of ridges and deeply cut valleys. Since the time the united monarchy of Israel divided into two kingdoms around 930 B.C. with Israel in the north and Judah in the south, Tekoa had a military garrison stationed there (2 Chron. 11:5-12; 17:2; 26:10). Therefore, Amos probably was quite aware of military activities that had taken place since the time of Rehoboam, who was the son of Solomon and the first king of the southern kingdom.

Evidence seems to suggest that Amos might have had more responsibilities than what a mere shepherd in the fields was accustomed to having. The word, *nōqēd*, is only used one other time in the Old Testament in 2 Kings 3:4. In this instance, the term apparently refers to the breeding and marketing of sheep and rams. The occupation is well documented in Mesopotamian history as one who was an overseer of herdsmen.[3] This understanding of the nature of Amos' occupation is consistent with his description of himself to Amaziah (7:10-17) where in 7:14 Amos calls himself a herdsman and one who tended sycamore trees. Perhaps the figs were somehow used as feed for his herds.[4] Whatever the specific nature of his work might have been, Amos labored in very common occupations for his time and place. In 7:10-17, Amos told Amaziah that these were his occupations and that he placed no special claim on holding the office of a prophet or having had training in the prophetic office previous to God's call. At one moment he had been minding his own businesses and in the next God had sent him from his home in Judah to Samaria in the northern kingdom to deliver God's Word to Israel.

---

3. Shalom Paul, *A Commentary on the Book of Amos,* Hermenia (Philadelphia: Fortress Press, 1991), 35-6.
4. T. J. Wright, 'Amos and the "Sycamore Fig",' *VT* 26 (1976): 368.

Amos' background should remind us of the kind of people God calls to His service. God calls people from a variety of backgrounds to serve Him, and many are called from very common backgrounds. Often, we might be tempted to believe that God only calls people who are especially gifted or talented to serve Him. A pastoral search committee would not have been very impressed by Amos' credentials (or lack thereof), and yet throughout the Scriptures we discover a God who does many extraordinary things through very ordinary people. Amos demonstrated a willingness to be obedient to God's call. He was very much aware of his own ordinary background, and he was more than ready to confess it to others. In fact, Amos might have experienced great joy in realizing that it was God who was sustaining him rather than his own abilities. Many of us in the church might say that we are inadequate to do what God has called us to do in His service. The truth is we are all inadequate. Jesus said, 'Apart from me you can do nothing' (John 15:5). Nevertheless, as the apostle Paul understood, we can do all things through Christ who strengthens us (Phil. 4:13). Instead of using his background and lack of formal training as an excuse to disobey God, Amos trusted and obeyed Him. There was nothing innately extraordinary about Amos himself except his faith in God and his faithfulness to God.

What may we know of Amos' setting?

A number of factors surrounding Amos' circumstances made his task more difficult than it already was. First, Amos lived in a time of *national disunity*. In 931 B.C., the northern tribes of Israel rebelled against King Rehoboam, King Solomon's son, and the nation of Israel split into two monarchies. The north retained the name Israel, and its first king was Jeroboam. The south called itself Judah since Judah was the name of that region since God had given it to the tribe of Judah at the time of the conquest. Rehoboam remained king in Judah. Since the split between the ten tribes of Israel in the north and the two tribes of Judah in the south, their history consisted of periodic seasons of civil war, unrest, and cooperation. Amos indicates that Jeroboam (II) was the king over Israel and that Uzziah was the king over Judah during his ministry. Jeroboam II reigned over Israel from about 793–753 B.C., and Uzziah reigned over Judah from about 792–740. Both the fathers of Jeroboam II and Uzziah had been at war with one another.

Jehoash was the father of Jeroboam II and had already been on the throne in Israel for about two or three years when Amaziah, Uzziah's father, came to the throne in Judah as the result of his father's assassination. Amaziah's first order of business was to establish control in his government by punishing those who had assassinated his father. Next, in order to protect his kingdom from a much more powerful threat to the north in Israel and to possibly regain territories that had been previously lost in the south, Amaziah began rebuilding Judah's military and fortifications. Apparently, Jeroboam and Amaziah initially got along with one another. Amaziah even hired mercenaries from Israel to help him in his campaign to recapture territory in the south from Edom (2 Chron. 25:5-13). However, the Lord was not pleased with Amaziah's hiring of these mercenaries since Israel had already rebelled against God. It was when Amaziah decided he no longer needed the Israelite mercenaries that tensions began to mount. As the mercenaries returned home they 'raided the cities of Judah, from Samaria to Beth-horon, and struck down 3,000 of them and plundered much spoil' (2 Chron. 25:13, NASB). Either there were a number of Judean settlements that existed in the north or Samaria and Beth-horon were the places from which these mercenaries attacked cities in the south. Either way, this turn of events certainly must have outraged Judah.

Having just accomplished a major victory over Edom, Amaziah believed he was ready to attack a more powerful Israel to his north. He sent a challenge to Jehoash to come and face him in battle. When Jehoash received the message he replied with a parable about a mighty cedar of Lebanon representing Israel and a scant thistle representing Judah. The thistle demanded that the great cedar provide its daughter as a bride for the thistle's son, but a mighty beast came and trampled the thistle into the ground. Jehoash warned Amaziah not to allow his victory over Edom to cloud his judgment and lead him to disaster in a war with Israel. However, Amaziah ignored Jehoash's warning and marched his army against Israel at Beth Shemesh. The Israelites routed Amaziah's army and Amaziah was captured and taken back to Jerusalem as Jehoash's prisoner. There, Amaziah watched as the Israelites destroyed a portion of the northern wall of Jerusalem and plundered the city, especially the temple and palace treasures (2 Chron. 25:21-24). Perhaps it was only the northern wall that they destroyed to demonstrate that Judah was powerless to defend themselves against their powerful enemy to the north. Moreover, Amaziah was taken back north to Samaria as Jehoash's prisoner (2 Kings 14:13-14). He was later released, probably at the time of Jehoash's death, since the author of 2 Chronicles clearly indicates that Amaziah lived fifteen years after the death of Jehoash. Jeroboam II and Uzziah both probably co-reigned with their fathers during the time these events occurred.[5]

After the deaths of Jehoash and Amaziah, Jeroboam II and Uzziah apparently never engaged in military hostilities toward one another. In fact, there seems to have been a spirit of cooperation that existed between the two monarchies.[6] Nevertheless, with the events that had taken place between their previous kings only some twenty years before, the sentiments between the people of Israel and Judah were probably mixed. Jehoash's parable of Israel as the great cedar of Lebanon while Judah was a mere thistle probably represented the northerners' attitudes toward those in the south, not only during his reign but also during the reign of his son. One might detect this attitude of superiority from Amaziah, the priest of Bethel, towards Amos (Amos 7:10-13). Also, Jehoash's march to Jerusalem was in many ways similar to Sherman's March to the Sea through Atlanta in the American Civil War. Nearly one hundred and fifty years later, one may still find those who resent the Northern States because of that incident. I have met people who act as if they are still fighting that war. Therefore, it is reasonable to assume that, while their leaders might have developed a spirit of political cooperation for the well-being of their respective monarchies, it would be naïve to assume there no longer existed any latent hostility between the peoples of the north and the south. All of this history is

---

5. Eugene H. Merrill, *Kingdom of Priests: A History of Old Testament Israel* (Grand Rapids: Baker Books, 2000), 370-4.
6. Thomas J. Finley, *An Exegetical Commentary: Joel, Amos, Obadiah* (Dallas: Biblical Studies Press, 2003), 102-3.

important, because Amos was from the south in Judah, and God called him to go north to Israel and preach a message of judgment. Amos, the southerner from Judah, the insignificant thistle, had the unsavory task of proclaiming a difficult message to an arrogant and less than receptive crowd in Israel, the mighty cedar of Lebanon to the north.

Second, Amos lived in a time of *military superiority*. For some time, Aram-Damascus had waged war on Israel, but in 802 B.C. the Assyrians conquered Damascus, and Israel enjoyed a time of relative peace. Nevertheless, a change in leadership and a new threat to the Assyrians caused them to relinquish their tight grip on Aram-Damascus, and once again the Arameans began acting aggressively toward Israel. Under King Jeroboam's rule, Israel prevailed against them. In fact, God blessed Israel's military so much that Israel expanded its borders in the north all the way to Hamath and Damascus and in the south as far as the Dead Sea in the Transjordan. Jeroboam had control of much of Lebanon, control of Aram-Damascus, control of Moab, and was confident of his superiority over Judah since his father had decidedly defeated her also. During the ministry of Amos, Israel was experiencing a time of strong national security. The prophet Jonah had prophesied that God would indeed increase the borders of Israel. However, God blessed Israel with this expansion and these military victories because of His mercy and grace on Israel even though Jeroboam 'did evil in the sight of Yahweh' (2 Kings 14:23-29).

Furthermore, even though Judah was less formidable than Israel, under Uzziah's leadership she too experienced military successes. Uzziah raised an army that numbered more than three hundred thousand men. He launched attacks against the Philistines to his west, against the Arabs to his south, and against the Meunites and Ammonites to his east. Judah was victorious in all of these military campaigns. Uzziah turned the defensive positions of his enemies into his own defensive positions thus strengthening his military even more. He also constructed impressive defences in and around Jerusalem. With the peace between Israel and Judah established, Judah had eliminated all of its threats to national security under Uzziah (2 Chron. 26:6-15). Between Israel and Judah, they nearly controlled as much land as they ever had, even when all of Israel had experienced its 'golden era' under Solomon. Third, along with these military advances a season of *economic prosperity* came for both Israel and Judah. Their economies flourished as new opportunities for trade opened up seemingly in every direction. A number of people in Israel's capital, Samaria, became very wealthy. They furnished their homes with exquisite wood and ivory furniture. The wealthy had the finest of foods and surroundings. Many were able to afford both winter and summer homes. In Judah, Uzziah was able to establish settlements in areas that had nearly been uninhabitable. It required amazing engineering and agricultural technology.[7] Not since the time of Solomon had so many in both the north and the south experienced such good fortune.

With the military successes that they experienced and the explosion of economic prosperity, no doubt many believed these happenings were a sign of God's favor. This conclusion would have arisen out of a naïve understanding of the Retribution Principle. The Retribution Principle is the basic understanding that when one obeys God He will bless them and when one disobeys God He will curse or punish them. Certainly it is true. Ultimately, God will bless those who obey Him, and He will judge those who disobey Him. However, God's blessing is no more a sure sign of God's pleasure than is difficulty in the life of an individual necessarily a sign of God's displeasure (cf. John 9:1-3). As we already observed, God blessed Jeroboam and Israel with increased borders, but it was in spite of the fact that Jeroboam had done evil in the sight of Yahweh.

According to Hosea and Amos, the people under Jeroboam were doing evil in the sight of Yahweh also. God's blessing came out of God's mercy and grace upon His chosen people. It had nothing to do with Israel's obedience to God. Perhaps, God did it in order to give them an opportunity to repent in the face of His lovingkindness. It was probably a matter much like the apostle Paul addressed when he wrote the church at Rome saying, 'do you think lightly of the riches of his kindness and tolerance and patience, not knowing that

---

7. Eugene H. Merrill, 'Agriculture in the Negev: An Exercise in Possibilitism,' *NEASB* 9 (1977): 25-35.

the kindness of God leads you to repentance? But because of your stubbornness and unrepentant heart you are storing up wrath for yourself in the day of wrath and revelation of the righteous judgment of God, who will render to each person according to his deeds' (Rom. 2:4-6, NASB). The people in Israel were storing up wrath for themselves in the day of judgment because of their stubbornness and unrepentant hearts even though they experienced God's kindness, tolerance, and patience. The Lord indicates that He even sent a number of hardships upon the people as well, but the calamities failed to drive the people back to Him (4:6-13).

If they had deceived themselves into thinking that God's blessing was the result of their obedience, then Amos would have had a difficult time convincing them otherwise. It is difficult for the wealthy to turn to God. Either they may see no need for God because life is as they want it, or they may see their wealth as a sign of His pleasure in them. It was to a people who felt more secure both militarily and financially than they had felt in quite a number of years that God sent Amos to preach a message of impending judgment and utter destruction—no easy task. Kaiser describes this period of Israel's history well, saying:

> In less than twenty-five years Jeroboam II was able to take a nation that was just about ready to die and turn it into one of the great powers of his day. The wealth and economic turn-around were so dramatic that it became a matter of concern for the prophets as they inveighed against those who 'adorned [their] houses with ivory,' both 'winter house' and' summer house' (Amos 3:15). In fact, so prosperous had they become that their wives were said to 'lie on beds inlaid with ivory and lounge on [their] couches ... din[ing] on choice lambs ... strum[ming] away on [their] harps like David and improvis[ing] on musical instruments, ... drink[ing] wine by the bowlful and us[ing] the finest lotions, but ... not [being] griev[ed] over the ruin of Joseph' (Amos 6:4-6). Hosea had warned as well (12:8) that 'Ephraim boasts, "I am rich; I have become wealthy. With all my wealth they will not find in me any iniquity or sin."' But Samaria, unknown to its inhabitants, was a 'fading flower,' whose 'glorious beauty' was about to be 'laid low' (Isa. 28:1).[8]

---

8. Walter C. Kaiser Jr., *A History of Israel: From the Bronze Age Through The Jewish Wars* (Nashville: Broadman & Holman Publishers, 1998), 352.

Fourth, Amos lived in a time of *religious activity*. He confronted a people who had developed a syncretistic approach to religion. It was a mixture of pagan idolatry alongside rituals and theological concepts taken from God's Word. Apparently, along with worshiping idols they were quite zealous in offering up worship to the Lord in the way of solemn assemblies, cultic feasts, worship songs, and tithes, and by observing the Sabbaths. Nevertheless, God was displeased with their hypocritical displays of worship. They clung to the words of Moses that best suited them. Israel knew they were God's chosen people. They remembered the Lord had brought them out of the bondage of Egypt. They knew they lived in the land that God had given them as their inheritance. They believed that they were enjoying the presence of the Lord just as they had since the days of Moses. They recognized God's judgment upon those who opposed them and continued to hope in God's protection from their enemies, anticipating the Day of the Lord when He would come and destroy their enemies. They counted on God's promise to Abram that He would be faithful to curse those who cursed them. Yet they had replaced sincere spirituality with insincere religiosity. Israel rejected righteousness and justice. The notion that they were sinful and in need of repentance was far from them. They had created an image of God in their minds that suited their purposes but contradicted reality. Their perverted theology and misrepresentation of God led to false hopes. They had deluded themselves into thinking that they were secure and right with God when, in fact, they were in danger and far from Him.

What may we know concerning his message?
Amos begins his message by identifying his source. This message originates with the Lord. Amos is but His messenger. What gives Amos authority is not his background or even the content of what he has to say, but it is the Lord Himself as Amos' source that gives authority to his message. The content of Amos' message is authoritative because it comes from God. Pastors and teachers of God's Word would do well to remember this truth today. What gives us authority is not our education, position, or talents, but it is God's call as He

has called us to be messengers proclaiming and teaching His authoritative Word. To stray from the Scriptures is to stray from God's call and message.

Furthermore, Amos uses the Hebrew covenantal name of God, Yahweh, as he reveals the source of his message.[9] Israel was an especially called people of God in a covenantal relationship with Yahweh. Yahweh had called their father Abraham out of a distant place in Ur of the Chaldeans to come to the land of Canaan, the land that became the location of the nation of Israel. Yahweh said that He would bless Abraham so that Abraham would be a blessing to the nations (Gen. 12:1-3). Yahweh delivered the people out of Egyptian bondage and established His covenant with the nation of Israel at Sinai where He said he would be their God and they would be His people. Yahweh established their nation and kept His promises to Abraham and their forefathers. He established the place where Israel was to worship Him on Mt Zion in Jerusalem. God manifested His presence in the midst of the nation at the temple in Jerusalem, the temple planned by David and built by Solomon. Amos' message comes from this God.

How does this message come? It comes with a roar. Why? It was because God's covenant with Israel involved responsibility and obedience. The Israelites were responsible to be faithful to Yahweh in obedience and service as His chosen people. According to God's law, if Israel would be loyal to Yahweh and worship Him only, then God would bless the nation. However, if they were to become disloyal to Yahweh and disobey His commandments and statutes, then they would be under the curse of God (Deut. 30:15-20). Yahweh's roar from Zion anticipates a word of judgment upon Israel because of her unfaithfulness. Amos poetically describes what Israel can expect as the result of God's judgment upon her. He begins by describing the results of a famine. While Amos' message nowhere else speaks of an actual famine coming upon the land, verse two describes what will happen to the land as a result of God's judgment. It will look as if a famine happened. Furthermore, Amos later speaks of a famine that will

---

9. Most modern translations of Scripture use 'Lord' to indicate the covenantal name for God, Yahweh, being employed in the Hebrew text.

Amos 1:1-2

come, not a famine where food is lacking but a famine where God's Word is lacking and nowhere to be found (8:11-14). It is possible that as Amos employs this poetic description of events to come he implies both meanings.[10]

STUDY QUESTIONS

1. What is significant about Amos' background?
2. How did Israel and Judah's disunity probably affect Amos' ministry?
3. What difficulties did Israel's military successes possibly pose as they heard Amos' message of judgment?
4. What difficulties did Israel's economic prosperity possibly pose as they heard Amos' message of judgment?
5. How did Israel's zealous religious practices become a problem for Israel?
6. How important was it for Amos to declare his message was from the Lord?
7. Why was Israel's unfaithfulness so serious?

---

10. See Isaiah's description of this time in Isaiah 1 and 5:7-25.

2

Judgment on Israel's Neighbors
(Amos 1:3–2:5)

Following the introduction, Amos begins with a series of pronouncements of judgment upon seven nations that surround Israel. Keep in mind that Amos' audience is Israel. He did not travel to these other nations to preach these decrees. These words were meant for the ears of the people in Israel. So why did Amos pronounce judgment on these other nations as he was addressing Israel? The pronouncements of judgment upon Israel's neighbors probably served several purposes.

First, they served as a means of getting his audience's attention. The Israelites had numerous past experiences with these other nations, and few of those experiences were positive. In fact, it is likely the Israelites had some hidden if not open hostility toward each of these nations, including Judah, with whom they had been at war just one generation before. Israel's relationship to their neighbors was much like an incident where a policeman involved in a dispute said, 'We had over 120 calls for service, 43 police reports, 20 of which went to the district attorney's office, and mutual restraining orders, all over a property line dispute. The disagreement had broadened over a three-year period to include not only the two male disputants but their wives, children and the neighborhood.' One disputant would call the police to complain about the other because he wanted him to pay for his unruly behavior, and then the other neighbor would follow

19

suit and do the same. Likewise, Israel believed its neighbors should pay for their sins. Usually, whenever a prophet spoke of God's judgment on other nations to God's people it was for the purpose of encouraging the people saying that God would either protect them or have vengeance on their enemies. As Amos began speaking of the atrocities committed by these nations along with God's judgment upon them, the people of Israel probably would have relished what they heard. Finally, these nations would be getting what they had coming to them.

Second, these pronouncements served to ensnare Israel by using their agreement with the notion that the sins of a nation should result in its judgment. If the sins of other nations demonstrate they deserve judgment, then Israel's sin demonstrates it deserves judgment too. Israel clearly saw the need for justice and the punishment of others who committed sin in which they had no part. However, Amos used their sense of outrage to suddenly have the point used against them. Amos used what one has deemed 'the rhetoric of entrapment.'[1] Another has said, 'In modern slang Amos, once he observed the shocked expressions on the listeners' faces, might have exclaimed, "Gotcha!"'[2]

Third, these pronouncements probably added some 'shock-value' to Amos' message and set the tone of what his audience could anticipate in the remainder of his message. It is interesting to note that Amos' pronouncements of judgment on the nations address seven nations that surrounded Israel. The number seven usually denotes completeness in the Scriptures. Therefore, when Amos reached his seventh nation, which just happened to be Judah, his audience was probably pleased to hear the judgment would be complete and that it would come to a climax upon Judah.[3] What's more, they possibly were surprised that Amos would speak in this way since he was from Judah. Imagine their shock when Amos continued with an eighth nation that had fallen under God's condemnation,

---

1. Robert Alter, *The Art of Biblical Poetry* (New York: Basic Books, 1985), 144.
2. Billy K. Smith, *Amos, Obadiah, Jonah*, in vol. 19B of *The New American Commentary*, ed. E. Ray Clendenen (Nashville: Broadman & Holman Publishers, 1995), 44.
3. Ibid., 44.

and that eighth nation was they themselves. Instead of being their protector, God would be Israel's adversary. It is usually easier for us to see the faults of others than to see our own. Furthermore, we tend to believe the sins of others are worse than our own.

Fourth, these pronouncements served as a reminder that God is sovereign over all nations and is the Judge of all nations that break His law. Some argue that the nations were wrongly judged because they had not been given God's law. How could God hold them responsible for breaking laws of which they were unaware? They had never heard of Moses, and God had never sent prophets to them. The Bible teaches that God has placed within all of us knowledge of right and wrong (Rom. 1:18-32; 2:14-15). As J. A. Motyer says: 'They were without special revelation but not without moral responsibility; they were without direct knowledge of God but not without accountability to God; they were without the law written upon tablets of stone but not without the law written in the conscience.'[4] The Lord holds each nation accountable for its inhumane treatment of others.

Fifth, these pronouncements indicate God's covenant with Israel did not make the Israelites immune to God's judgment. On the contrary, since God had chosen Israel out of all the nations to be a holy nation He held His people to a higher standard. To him who is given much, much is required. Israel had heard God's messengers and had seen His power manifested many times in various ways. Therefore, God expected more from His people, and because of this relationship to Israel the consequences of their sin would be greater.

Sixth, these pronouncements demonstrate God's patience with sinners. Reading these verses one might think they convey anything but God's patience. Yet, His judgment comes after continued and prolonged sinful activities. When Amos says 'for three transgressions ... even for four', he is stressing the following: (1) these nations have been repeatedly sinning, (2) the addition of 3 + 4 being 7 suggests the cumulative nature of their sin that has reached a place that demands

---

4. J. A. Motyer, *The Message of Amos: The Day of the Lion*, in *The Bible Speaks Today*, ed. J. A. Motyer (Downers Grove, IL: Inter-Varsity Press, 1974), 37.

judgment,[5] and (3) the phrase may suggest that if three sins tried the Lord's patience, then four was more than He would tolerate.[6] There comes a point where enough is enough, even with God. Given the nature of the sins mentioned in these pronouncements one might wonder why God allowed these nations to get away with what they had been doing for so long. When I wonder why God seems so slow to take action against those I believe deserve God's judgment I am reminded of how glad I am that God is patient with sinners, considering my own fallen nature. God's default response is not wrath and judgment but mercy and grace. Even so, there may come a point when people's hearts can become so hardened against God that they become utterly unresponsive to Him, and God's judgment is 'irrevocable.'[7]

Seventh, these pronouncements of judgment upon Israel's neighbors reveal God's concern for how people treat others, especially those who are weak and defenceless. These nations committed terrible atrocities. They brutally slaughtered defenseless prisoners of war. They were guilty of human trafficking, taking advantage of others for profit. They broke their commitments to others. They killed women and unborn children. They displayed contempt for others as they desecrated their dead. While God is opposed to all sin, He is especially opposed to those who take advantage of others and are lacking in human decency. Those who do such things will be punished. This theme reappears often in the book of Amos. Quoting the Old Testament law, Jesus said that not only are we to love God, but we are to love our neighbor as ourselves. Amos' message makes known just how serious God is when it comes to loving our neighbor and the consequences of our failure to do so.

- 1:3-5   – treating people as if they have no worth
- 1:6-8   – using people for profit
- 1:9-10 – breaking one's word to a brother in order to use him for a profit
- 1:11-12 – unrestrained hatred and spite toward a brother
- 1:13-15 – ambition and uncontrolled violence against the helpless

---

5. Finley, 127-8.
6. Michael L. Barré, 'The Meaning of *l'šybnw* in Amos 1:3–2:6,' *JBL* 105 (1986): 621.
7. See Hebrews 5:11–6:8; 10:26; 12:16-17.

2:1-3 – showing contempt for others
2:4-5 – unfaithfulness to God and His Word

Damascus: Treating People as if They Have No Worth (1:3-5)

Damascus was the strongest and most formidable city-state in Aram, located northeast of Israel. For nearly a hundred years the Arameans were one of Israel's greatest enemies. Gilead was a very fertile area and was the Israelite region located east of the Jordan River not far from Aram. Therefore, on numerous occasions Aram invaded this territory in efforts to expand its empire. Under King Hazael, the Arameans confiscated the Israelite regions east of the Jordan River and apparently forced Israel to become their vassal (2 Kings 10:32-33). Not long after, Judah also became a vassal of Aram (2 Kings 12:17-18). As a result, Aram became a noteworthy empire during the mid to late ninth century B.C.[8] This domination over Israel and Judah continued under Hazael's son, Ben-Hadad. Nevertheless, with Aram having to defend itself against the Assyrians to Aram's northeast, King Jehoash (798–782) of Israel was able to repossess the cities Hazael had taken (2 Kings 13:25). Under Jehoash's son, King Jeroboam II, Israel was able to reclaim all the territory it had lost to the Arameans (2 Kings 14:25-27). Jeroboam's conquest happened while Amos was living.

Amos reveals the sin of the Arameans; it was the brutal treatment of their Israelite prisoners when Aram had invaded Gilead. He says the Arameans will experience God's judgment because they 'threshed Gilead with sledges having iron teeth' (NIV). 'Threshed' refers to the process of separating seed from the stalk. The process often involved an animal walking back and forth over the harvested grain pulling a heavy sledge that was curved upward at the front along with knifelike iron prongs driven through it. Amos describes an atrocity when the Arameans drove animals pulling these sledges over their prostrate Israelite captives. Some suggest this description should not be taken literally but as a descriptive way of conveying the cruelty of

---

8. Wayne T. Pitard, 'Arameans' in *Peoples of the Old Testament World*, eds. Alfred J. Hoerth, Gerald L. Mattingly, and Edwin M. Yamauchi (Grand Rapids: Baker Book House, 1994), 218-20.

the Arameans when they invaded Gilead.⁹ However, given the excessive brutality common to warfare in that day, the hatred between Israel and Aram, and the fact that the rest of the accounts of the other nations' sins seem to be literal, there is every reason to accept this description literally as well. Either way, Amos makes his point. Aram probably committed numerous brutal atrocities against the Israelites, and Amos' description probably provided a vivid picture summarizing them. What's more, God was holding Damascus accountable for these atrocities. Motyer aptly describes the heart of the matter:

> War or no war, Hazael had no liberty to treat people as if they were things. It is the first absolute moral principle for which Amos campaigns: people are not things. Let us suppose that the description of Hazael's conduct as 'threshing' Gilead does not actually mean that he used animals to drag flint-studded, weighted platforms of wood back and forth across prostrate bodies of living Gileadites. Take it metaphorically, but ask what the metaphor means. 'Threshing' is what a man does to a thing, a grain crop, in order to extract his own profit from it. This is what Hazael did in Gilead. He treated people as things. But found no sympathy, allowance or forgiveness in heaven.¹⁰

Although people may show a disregard for human life, they may not claim any valid excuse for such action.

Therefore, their destruction was sure. God Himself would wage war on the Arameans, apparently beginning with Damascus, the most prominent city-state of Aram, and then moving on to the Valley of Aven, meaning 'the valley of wickedness', and to Beth Eden, literally 'the house of pleasure.' These were probably two more Aramean city-states. Fire was a common instrument of war because of its power to consume, and a broken gate indicated the enemy could easily come in to destroy a city.¹¹ God used the Assyrians as His instrument of destruction as they totally decimated the cities and lands of Aram and carried its people off into exile. Anyone who treats people as things of no value will not escape God's judgment.

---

9. D. A. Hubbard, *Joel and Amos*, Tyndale Old Testament Commentaries (Downers Grove: InterVarsity Press, 1989), 131.
10. Motyer, 39-40.
11. Smith, 49.

Gaza: Using People for Profit (1:6-8)

Another long-time enemy of Israel were the Philistines. They came and settled in the southwest portion of Palestine in the early twelfth century B.C. It was not long before they had established a pentapolis of five city-states in the region made up of Gaza, Ashkelon, Ashdod, Ekron, and Gath. This confederation of Philistine city-states became a major power in the region until about 1000 B.C., the time of David.[12] The Philistines were astute warriors, with strong iron weapons and chariots, accompanied by a desire to expand their territory. Therefore, as they moved eastward into the foothills of the central hill country of Canaan they came into conflict with the Israelites.

It was this military conflict that served as a catalyst for Israel's establishment of a monarchy.[13] As the first king of Israel, King Saul's prime directive was to defeat the Philistines, but it was the Philistines who killed both Saul and his son, Jonathan. In fact, they cut off Saul's head, pinned his body and his son's body on the city wall of Bethshan, and paraded his head around the cities of Philistia. This was the beginning of a long-standing animosity between Israel and Philistia. After King David finally defeated them, the Philistines continued to prosper as they controlled two of the most important trade routes in the entire ancient Near East. One called 'the way of the sea' ran along the Mediterranean coast from Egypt in the south up to the land of the Hittites in the north, which is present-day Turkey. It connected with the major routes going east to Mesopotamia. The second ran west to east from the Mediterranean coast to Edom and connected to the King's Highway that ran up the Transjordanian plateau. During the time of the Divided Monarchy, Philistia continued to be a menace to Israel and Judah.[14] Consequently, the Israelites during Amos' day no doubt continued to harbor a deeply seated hostility toward the Philistines.

Like the Arameans, the Philistines also treated others as objects or things but with a major difference. While the Arameans

---

12. William H. Stiebing, Jr. *Ancient Near Eastern History and Culture* (New York: Addison Wesley Longman, Inc., 2003), 252.
13. David M. Howard, 'Philistines,' in *Peoples of the Old Testament World*, eds. Alfred J. Hoerth, Gerald L. Mattingly, and Edwin M. Yamauchi (Grand Rapids: Baker Book House, 1994), 240-1.
14. See 1 Kings 15:27; 16:15-18; 2 Chronicles 17:11; 21:16-17.

treated others as objects with no value, the Philistines treated others as objects to be exploited for their value. Their sin was the capture of entire towns and villages for the sole purpose of turning a profit as they sold their captives into slavery. These raids probably had nothing to do with being at war with another nation. They seemed to be for the sole purpose of kidnapping people in order to turn a profit. Their actions were much like the slave traders of early America who went to Africa and captured entire villages, enslaved them, and then sold them for a profit. The Philistines saw other people as objects of personal gain; they dealt in human trafficking. Their biggest concern was how much they could get out of these people.

At first glance, we may think of pimps using young women as prostitutes as a modern example of such abuse and be glad that most of us never come into contact with such exploitation. Then again, upon further contemplation, we see that there are more common, 'acceptable' ways in which this happens. Whenever an employer fails to pay his employees a fair wage for services rendered, it is a subtle form of wrongfully using others for personal profit. I am reminded of when I was a boy and I was trading baseball cards with another boy. I offered him some cards that I knew were worth very little for a card that had a great deal of value. I knew he liked the players I was offering him, but I also knew that it was not a fair deal. My concern was not fairness; my concern was to use him to get what I wanted. Ironically and justly, over time the cards I traded him gained more value than the one I got from him in the trade. Taking advantage of others for our own profit is the sin Amos addressed. To be guilty of such exploitation is to be guilty of treating people made in the image of God as mere commodities.[15] Furthermore, Amos makes it clear that God will not allow such actions to go unpunished. We always tread on thin ice when we value things more than we value people.

Tyre: Breaking One's Word to a Brother in Order to Use Him for a Profit (1:9-10)
The city of Tyre was located on the Mediterranean coast north of Israel, in what is modern Lebanon, and it controlled most of

---

15. B. K. Smith, 51.

Phoenicia during the time of Amos.[16] The Phoenicians were of Canaanite origin, but their unique culture distinguished them from their neighbors and ancestors.[17] They were a seafaring people whose economy depended on their exporting and importing of goods. The Phoenicians often served as the 'middlemen' in the trading of all manner of commodities including slaves. It is possible they were in collusion with Gaza and Edom's slave trade. About one hundred and fifty years later the prophet Joel brought up the fact that the nations had joined together in a cooperative effort in selling slaves (Joel 3:4-8).[18]

Nevertheless, even though Tyre might have played a smaller role than that of others in the trading of slaves, they were no less guilty of treating people made in God's image as things and exploiting them for profit. In addition, as appalling as that sin was, their wickedness went deeper because the very people they sold were their friends. Their debauchery was intensified by their treachery. Apparently, Tyre had turned on someone with whom it had made a treaty or covenant of peace. It is possible that this betrayal was perpetrated against Israel. Since the time of David and Solomon, Israel seems to have had very close relations with Tyre (1 Kings 5:12). In fact, King Ahab's marriage to Jezebel surely entered Israel into a covenant with the Phoenicians (1 Kings 16:31). Such covenants made the parties involved 'brothers' (1 Kings 9:13), an expression used to describe a close relationship characterized by love and loyalty.[19] There is no record of a war between Israel and Tyre. Nonetheless, Psalm 83 indicates Tyre was among a coalition of nations surrounding Israel that conspired against God's people. If it were Israel whom Tyre betrayed, Amos' inclusion of Tyre's sin in his address to Israelites would make sense. Some have suggested that Tyre actually turned against another Phoenician city, and Amos' mention of this disloyalty

---

16. Walther Eichrodt, *Ezekiel: A Commentary*, Old Testament Library (Philadelphia: Westminster, 1970), 12.
17. William A. Ward, 'Phoenicians,' in *Peoples of the Old Testament World*, eds. Alfred J. Hoerth, Gerald L. Mattingly, and Edwin M. Yamauchi (Grand Rapids: Baker Book House, 1994), 184.
18. Gary V. Smith, *Hosea, Amos, Micah,* The NIV Application Commentary (Grand Rapids: Zondervan Publishing House, 2001), 241.
19. B. K. Smith, 53.

to a brother demonstrates God's concern for people everywhere and not just for Israel.[20] Either way the people of Tyre were traitors. Whether Tyre victimized Israel or someone else, the Lord would hold them responsible for the exploitation of their brothers. The Assyrians and Babylonians brought Tyre under submission several times.

Edom: Unrestrained Hatred and Spite Toward a Brother (1:11-12)

Edom had an unusual relationship with Israel. On the one hand, the biblical writers often referred to Edom as Israel's 'brother.' The Lord told the Israelites, 'You shall not abhor an Edomite, for he is your brother' (Deut. 23:7). This relationship went back to Jacob and Esau who were brothers. The descendants of Jacob became the nation of Israel, and the descendants of Esau became the nation of Edom. On the other hand, since the time of Jacob and Esau the relationship between their descendants was strained at best and was more commonly one of open hostility. From the beginning of Israel's monarchy its kings went to battle against Edom. Saul fought against the Edomites and inflicted heavy casualties upon them (1 Sam. 14:47), but it was David who brought them under complete subjugation during his reign (2 Sam. 8:13-14). As Solomon's reign came to a close Edom rebelled against Israel and eventually won its independence during the time of Jehoram, Judah's king (2 Kings 8:20-22). The prophet Obadiah's message addressed an incident that occurred during this ongoing conflict as he pronounced judgment against Edom because of its offences against God's people.

In this instance, Amos confronts Edom's sin of pursuing 'his brother with the sword'. Since the writers of the Old Testament often refer to the Israelites and Edomites as brothers, it is likely Amos is addressing an incident that involved these two nations. Another possibility for Amos' use of the term 'brother' is the same as how he may have used it earlier in verse nine, meaning a treaty-partner.[21] In this case,

---

20. Roy L. Honeycutt, *Amos and His Message: An Expository Commentary* (Nashville: Broadman Press, 1963), 24.
21. M. Fishbane, 'The Treaty Background of Amos 1:11 and Related Matters,' *JBL* 89 (1970): 314-15.

the recipient of Edom's wrongdoing would be unknown. However, since the Old Testament often speaks of Edom as Israel and Judah's brother, it is likely this relationship is what he has in mind, and it would have been Amos' audience that had been the recipients of Edom's cruelty. Furthermore, since there was an ongoing antagonism between the Israelites and the Edomites, it is difficult to pinpoint for certain what is the specific incident of which Amos is speaking.

The phrase 'cast off all pity' or 'stifled his compassion' (NASB) is a little ambiguous in its original language of Hebrew. Consequently, it may be understood in a number of ways. First, it could mean the Edomites ignored the natural affections one should have toward one's own family. This understanding of the phrase seems to be the prevailing one we find in most English translations. Second, the phrase could be translated 'destroyed his allies,' a translation that corresponds nicely to the preceding phrase if one understands 'brother' to be a treaty-partner.[22] A third possibility may be to understand the phrase as 'he did violence to his women,' following the example of Judges 5:30. If this is the correct understanding of the phrase, then it is referring to the infliction of sexual violence and physical harm on Israel's women by Edomite soldiers. Given the parallelism of the passage and the actual usage of these words in Hebrew, this third interpretation appears to make the most sense.[23] Hence, Amos is describing the complete suffering and subjugation of God's people to the cruelty and brutality of the Edomites. These atrocities were executed not only on the men who would have defended themselves but also upon defenseless women. What happened is similar to the masses who were killed by the Nazis in Russia, many of whom were elderly and women and children, or to the numerous women who became the objects of Russian soldiers' rage and vengeance when they captured Berlin in World War II. God is concerned not only with how we as individuals treat our enemies but with how nations treat their enemies too.

Why did Edom commit such horrific acts? It is because 'his anger raged continually' (NIV) and 'his fury stormed un-

---

22. Michael Barré, 'Amos 1:11 Reconsidered,' *CBQ* 47 (1985): 420-7.
23. Paul, 64-5; Duane A. Garrett, *Amos A Handbook on the Hebrew Text* (Waco: Baylor University Press, 2008), 39-40.

checked.' It is as if the hatred of the Edomites continued to fuel itself until it was totally out of control. I have witnessed people work themselves up into a frenzy as they continued to vent their anger about someone else. Instead of 'getting it off of their chest,' so to speak, they only managed to nurture their hatred and allow it to grow. For this reason, the Scriptures warn us about allowing bitterness and anger to overcome us: 'Whoever is slow to anger is better than the mighty, and he who rules his spirit than he who takes a city' (Prov. 16:32); 'Make no friendship with a man given to anger, nor go with a wrathful man, lest you learn his ways and entangle yourself in a snare' (Prov. 22:24-25); 'Let all bitterness and wrath and anger and clamor and slander be put away from you, along with all malice' (Eph. 4:31); 'See to it that no one fails to obtain the grace of God; that no "root of bitterness" springs up and causes trouble, and by it many become defiled' (Heb. 12:15). Instead of uprooting its bitterness toward its brother, Edom nurtured it until it became an uncontrolled inferno that resulted in devastation upon Israel and judgment upon Edom.

Amos describes how God's judgment will come upon Edom. Just as Edom's anger blazed against its brother so the Lord would send fire down upon Edom as enemies would come and torch their lands and cities. Teman and Bozrah appear to have been prominent districts in the south and north of Edom respectively. They were the main centers of power in Edom. God's judgment, therefore, would be wide-ranging (as it encompassed Edom's lands) and devastating (as it brought down Edom's foundations of financial and military security). As profound as the depth of Edom's sin was against its brother, so God's judgment would be upon Edom.

Ammon: Ambition and Uncontrolled Violence Against the Helpless (1:13-15)
As with Edom, the Israelites were distant relatives of the Ammonites. The Ammonites were descendants of Lot, Abraham's nephew, by way of an incestuous relationship between Lot and his younger daughter. The child's name was Ben-ammi (Gen. 19:30-38). The Ammonites lived in a cramped area between Moab to the south, Israel in Gilead to the west, Aram to the north, and the Syro-Arabian Desert to the east.

At that time, as throughout much of history, nations believed increasing their borders demonstrated power and prestige to neighboring kingdoms. In the Bible, the people of God saw it as a blessing upon their nation (2 Kings 14:25-27; Isa. 26:15).[24] Therefore, the limited amount of land that belonged to the Ammonites, along with their desire to make stronger their political position with their neighbors, appeared to have made them eager to expand whenever the opportunity afforded itself to do so.

The Israelites had a long history with the Ammonites. When the Israelites were initially entering the Promised Land, God instructed them to leave the land of the Ammonites alone because he had given it to Lot and his descendants as their inheritance (Deut. 2:19). Nevertheless, the history between these two peoples is one of hostility and bloodshed. On numerous occasions the Ammonites either joined other nations in attacks against Israel and Judah or opposed God's people on their own. The kings of Israel and Judah had many battles with the Ammonites.[25]

In this instance, Amos condemns the Ammonites for an incident when their ambition to increase their borders into Gilead led to the most heinous acts of brutality: the ripping open of the bellies of pregnant women. This hideous crime against humanity was not unheard of in the ancient Near East. Assyrian and Babylonian inscriptions mention the practice in their records of battles.[26] For instance, the Assyrian king, Tiglath-Pileser III speaking of one of his conquests said, he 'slit the wombs of the pregnant women, he gouged out the eye of the infants, he cut the throats of their young men.'[27] Furthermore, the Old Testament mentions it on three other occasions. First, Elisha prophesied the Arameans would rip open the bellies of pregnant women and dash to pieces their infants (2 Kings 8:12). Second, Menahem, the king of Israel,

---

24. Jeff Niehaus, 'Amos,' in *The Minor Prophets* vol. 1, ed. Thomas McComiskey (Grand Rapids: Baker Book House, 1992), 354.
25. See for example Judges 3:12-14; 10:6–11:33; 1 Samuel 11:1-11; 2 Samuel 8:12; 10:1-14; 12:31; 2 Kings 24:1-3; 2 Chronicles 20:1-30; 27:5; Nehemiah 4:1-3; Zephaniah 2:8-11.
26. Paul, 68.
27. M. Cogan, '"Ripping Open Pregnant Women" in Light of an Assyrian Analogue,' *JAOS* 103 (1983): 755-7.

committed this atrocity against his own people in the Israelite city of Tiphsah and in its surrounding region because of their lack of submission to him (2 Kings 15:16). Third, Hosea prophesied this act of viciousness along with the dashing of infants into pieces would happen in Israel at the fall of its capital, Samaria (Hosea 13:16). Such acts of brutality appear to have been common in the ancient Near East, instilling fear into the hearts of one's enemies and minimizing the chances of reprisals from later generations.[28]

It is difficult to pinpoint the exact time this incident happened since Israel and Ammon had such a long history of conflict. It has been suggested the Ammonites coordinated their attacks with Damascus when it invaded Gilead from the north, 'subjecting Gilead to a pincer movement' (Amos 1:3).[29] This suggestion is logical given the Ammonites propensity to join other nations attacking Israel and Judah at other times (Judg. 3:12-14; 2 Kings 24:1-3). Whenever the incident took place, God was going to exact judgment on the Ammonites as they gratified their lust for conquest and expansion through their ruthlessness upon the weak and helpless. Kings of that era may have thought such brutality was an effective way to wage war, but the Lord condemned the Ammonites for their crimes against those who could not defend themselves. Nothing gives rise to God's vengeance any more than senseless brutality committed upon those who are defenceless.

Amos' Israelite audience, no doubt, was eager to witness God's judgment exacted upon the Ammonites. Amos foresaw the destruction of their capital city, Rabbah (present-day Amman, Jordan). The Lord's judgment will come in the way of fire upon its fortifications amid the chaos and cries of battle. The Ammonites will find themselves in the whirlwind of a great storm as their enemies bring about this devastation upon them. In the end, Ammon's king and his officials will all go into exile. Those who exacted hideous crimes against the helpless will find themselves helpless. Those who treated defenseless women and unborn children with disdain will themselves be herded like cattle to a foreign land by others who show them no regard or sympathy. God used the Assyrians and the Babylonians to subdue Ammon,

---

28. See 1 Kings 11:14-16.
29. Hubbard, 136.

and it was probably Nebuchadnezzar's attacks that brought an end to Ammon's status as an independent kingdom.[30] One of the last records of the Ammonites is of their defeat by Judas Maccabees (1 Macc. 5:6-7).

Moab: Showing Contempt for Others (2:1-3)
Like the Ammonites, the Moabites were distant relatives of the Israelites. Moab was the product of Lot's incestuous relationship with his older daughter (Gen. 19:30-38). The relationship between Israel and Moab mostly was one of open hostility and conflict. When Moses led the Israelites through the Transjordan as they neared Canaan, Balak, the Moabite king, hired Balaam to curse the Israelites because he feared the threat they posed to his kingdom. When Balaam's attempts failed, Moabite women went into Israel's camp and enticed them to worship Baal of Peor and sexually seduced them into acts of immorality. The Lord punished Israel for its unfaithfulness by slaying twenty-four thousand Israelites (Num. 22–25). When Israel settled in the Promised Land, the tribes of Reuben and Gad inhabited the region just north of Moab. Their settlement in this region became a source of contention between these two tribes and Moab.[31] During the time of the judges Israel came under Moabite rule for eighteen years until Ehud liberated Israel when he killed Moab's King Eglon (Judg. 3:12-30).

From the beginning of Israel's establishment of a monarchy its kings conducted military operations against Moab. Saul fought with Moab (1 Sam. 14:47), and David subdued Moab and made it his vassal (2 Sam. 8:2). Mesha, the Moabite king, paid tribute to Israel's King Ahab, but when Ahab died, Mesha rebelled against Ahab's son, Jehoram. With the help of Judah and Edom, Jehoram defeated Mesha (2 Kings 1:1; 3:1-27). It is possible when Mesha recuperated from this defeat he exacted reprisals against Edom. If so, Amos may have been referring to this time in his indictment of Moab. It would have happened about ninety years before Amos.

---

30. Randall W. Younker, 'Ammonites,' in *Peoples of the Old Testament World*, eds. Alfred J. Hoerth, Gerald L. Mattingly, and Edwin M. Yamauchi (Grand Rapids: Baker Book House, 1994), 314.
31. Gerald L. Mattingly, 'Moabites,' in *Peoples of the Old Testament World*, eds. Alfred J. Hoerth, Gerald L. Mattingly, and Edwin M. Yamauchi (Grand Rapids: Baker Book House, 1994), 326.

What was Moab's sin? Amos says Moab 'burned to lime the bones of the king of Edom'. This act demonstrated Moab's deep hatred and absolute scorn for Edom. Not only did the Moabites show total disrespect to Edom's king, they rendered worthless the people of Edom as well. Just as a nation's flag today represents the nation, in the ancient Near East the king was the symbol of the nation. In fact, even today one might visit a nation where there are large images of the nation's leader displayed in prominent places. In these instances, the people's allegiance to the leader often is equated to their allegiance to the nation. The Moabites used the bones of Edom's king as an ingredient in the making of plaster used to whitewash their walls. The Moabites' message was clear: 'The worth of an Edomite is the same as the lime we use to whitewash our walls.' Their act was to dehumanize the Edomites and portray them as of no value. In 1993, I recall watching on the television the image of a mob in Mogadishu dragging the corpse of an American soldier through the dirty streets of that city. As an American, emotions of anger and revulsion welled up inside of me as I realized the utter contempt these people were showing not only to this man and his family, but to every American this soldier represented. Amos is denouncing such horrendous acts of dehumanization and disregard of others. Such crimes against humanity will bring about God's condemnation and wrath. These acts are not only sins against humanity who was created in God's image, but against God Himself. Amos' message indicates God will judge those who commit such acts of indecency whether they are perpetrated on God's elect or upon anyone else. There is a common sense of morality all people share as persons made in the image of God, and God will hold us all accountable to it.

As the Moabites were guilty of 'burning' the bones of the Edomite king, so they too will experience 'burning' as the Lord will send burning upon Moab. The fire will consume the fortifications of Kerioth, one of Moab's foremost cities. Amos describes the battle depicting Moab's demise, and the last sounds Moab will hear will be the blasts of trumpets of warfare and their enemies' triumphant shouts of victory. The decimation will be complete, as Moab's king, along with all his officials, will perish. The Assyrians laid ruin Moab on numerous occasions, but it was King Nebuchadnezzar of Babylon who destroyed Moab once and for all in 582 B.C.[32]

Judah: Unfaithfulness to God and His Word (2:4-5)
Amos' pronouncement concerning Judah might surprise some people in a number of ways. First, it might be surprising that Judah is included on this list since the rest of the list consists of heathen nations. After all, Judah is part of God's elect. Its relationship to the Lord and, more importantly, the Lord's relationship to Judah were significantly different from God's relationship with the other nations. Judah was part of God's 'treasured possession among all peoples' (Exod. 19:5). However, Amos' indictment of Judah indicates no one is exempt from the consequences of one's responsibilities and actions before God, regardless of one's standing.

Second, one might be surprised by Judah's inclusion on this list since the nature of Judah's sin appears to be so glaringly different from the inhumanities perpetrated by the other nations. We have seen extremely disturbing acts of degradation, treachery, indecency, and brutality meted out by the other nations on this list. Judah's sins of despising the Lord's instruction, of failing to keep His statutes, and of following after falsehoods, therefore, may sound somewhat less serious than those of the other nations. Of course it is important to embrace God's instruction, to obey His statutes, and to live in accordance to His truth. But how can failure in these matters compare to the atrocities committed by the heathen nations on Amos' list?

Actually, the accusations against Judah are more severe than the pronouncements of judgment levied against the other nations. The other nations acted against God's revelation of a common conscience we all have as creatures made in the image of God, but Judah had more. Judah had a history of God's revealed presence and mighty deeds in their midst. They had a history of prophets who proclaimed God's Word to them. Moreover, they had the blessing of being in a unique covenant relationship with the Lord who had saved them as His treasured possession and a holy nation. At the center

---

32. Ibid., 328.

of this covenant was the Law. The Hebrew word for 'law' or 'instruction' is *tôrâ*. The rejection of the Lord's *tôrâ* and His statutes was a rejection of the covenant God had made with His people at Mt Sinai. Therefore, it was the rejection of the Lord Himself. B. K. Smith explains *tôrâ* well:

> It is the embodiment of justice and righteousness and may be equated with the knowledge of God, the rejection of which results and consists in all manner of religious and social wickedness and amounts to breaking the covenant. For Judah to reject the Lord's instruction was comparable to the atrocities committed by foreign nations.[33]

The breaking of the Lord's covenant by His people had farther-reaching consequences than did the sins of the other nations. Exodus 19:4-8 reveals God's purpose for saving Israel and establishing a covenant with her. God saved His people so that they would become a 'kingdom of priests'. Just as the priests of Israel were mediators between Israel and the Lord, making it possible for God's people to draw near to God, so Israel's purpose was to show the nations the way to God.

Second, Israel was called into a covenant with the Lord to be a holy nation, setting themselves apart from all other gods as they worshipped and faithfully served the one true and living God. It was to be through their faithful obedience and holiness as God's chosen people that He would use them as His instrument of blessing and witness to the nations.[34] The rejection of the Lord's covenant by His people not only concerned them but every nation. The covenant God made with Israel was part of His eternal purpose of redeeming a people to Himself from every nation. Consequently, the sins of Judah and the sins of Israel, which will be Amos' focus for the remainder of the book, are far greater than the sins of the other nations. As Jesus says, 'And that servant who knew his master's will but did not get ready or act according to his will, will receive a severe beating. But the one who did not know, and did what deserved a beating, will receive a light beating. Everyone to whom much was given, of him much will be

---

33. B. K. Smith, 59.
34. See Genesis 12:1-3; Isaiah 43:8-13.

required, and from him to whom they entrusted much, they will demand the more' (Luke 12:47-48). Note Judah's digression into sin. First, the people consciously rejected God's covenant of grace and love in their hearts. Moses warned of rejecting the covenant and becoming one who 'blesses himself in his heart, saying, "I shall be safe, though I walk in the stubbornness of my heart"' (Deut. 29:19). Open rebellion against God begins with the hidden rejection of his Word in one's heart. It is for this reason the psalmist expresses his commitment to God's Word, saying, 'How can a young man keep his way pure? By guarding it according to your word. With my whole heart I seek you; let me not wander from your commandments! I have stored up your word in my heart, that I might not sin against you' (Ps. 119:9-11). Motyer speaks to the importance of God's Word to God's people when he writes:

> Here is a very largely forgotten and yet most vital principle. It is certainly the case that the church is called by God to safeguard, publicize and transmit His truth (*e.g.* 2 Tim. 1:13, 14; 2:1, 2); but it is equally the case that the truth is the safeguard of the church, both in the corporate sense of preserving the whole body and in the individual sense of guarding, defending and keeping each member. The life which walks in the truth is impregnable (*cf.* John 8:31, 32, 34-36).[35]

Having God's Word is no substitute for embracing God's Word. The people in Amos' day had possession of God's Word, but they did not embrace it like the psalmist did. From time to time I have heard people in the United States debate having the Ten Commandments on display in public places. While I think believers need to proclaim and display God's Word in the world today, I wonder how many of us are more concerned about putting God's Word on display than we are about embracing it in our lives as a witness to the world. We must not be as those James describes who look into God's Word and then forget it. Instead, we need to be doers of the Word; only then will it protect us from sin and its consequences (James 1:22-25).

---

35. Motyer, 54.

If open rebellion against God begins with the hidden rejection of God's Word in the heart, it is just as true the hidden rejection of God's Word in the heart will eventually lead to open rebellion against God. Such was the case in the time of Amos. It is impossible to believe one thing and yet do another. The fruit of one's life indicates what is in one's heart. The Lord Jesus says: 'For from within, out of the heart of man, come evil thoughts, sexual immorality, theft, murder, adultery, coveting, wickedness, deceit, sensuality, envy, slander, pride, foolishness. All these evil things come from within, and they defile a person' (Mark 7:21-23). Judah's open disobedience to God's statutes was consistent with and a result of their rejection of his *tôrâ*, their rejection of the Lord Himself.

Judah had been the recipient of the truth, God's Word. Instead of living in the way of God's Word, the people chose to walk the path of lies. Even though their history was full of examples where their fathers had followed this path to destruction, they chose to travel down the same road. The heritage we leave our children can have a strong impact on their lives. We should ask ourselves if our children hear us speak of commitment to Christ while at the same time witness our failure to truly live each day in that commitment. Are we merely possessors and professors of God's Word, or have we embraced it as the Lord Jesus Christ has embraced us? Some might say this notion smacks of bibliolatry, making an idol of God's Word. If so, they need to read Psalm 119. The person who has a deep love for the Lord will have a profound passion for His Word, to know it and to live it.

Like their fathers before them, the people of Judah were intoxicated by the lies of false prophets, and the people chose either to ignore God's Word or to pervert it to suit their own ends. Paul warned Timothy of false prophets saying, 'I charge you in the presence of God and of Christ Jesus, who is to judge the living and the dead, and by his appearing and his kingdom: preach the word; be ready in season and out of season; reprove, rebuke, and exhort, with complete patience and teaching. For the time is coming when people will not endure sound teaching, but having itching ears they will accumulate for themselves teachers to suit their own passions, and will turn away from listening to the truth and wander off into myths. As for you, always be sober-minded, endure suffering, do the work of an evangelist, fulfil your ministry' (2 Tim. 4:1-5). Believers must be ever mindful of the threat posed by false prophets lest we become like Judah. Judah followed the way of the false prophets to its bitter end with total disregard for the *torâ*.[36] Near the time of Amos' prophetic ministry, King Uzziah of Judah was an excellent example of Judah's rejection of the Lord's *torâ*. He disregarded the warning of the Lord's priests, entered the Temple, and offered incense on the altar, a duty only the priests were to perform according to the *torâ*. The Lord struck Uzziah with leprosy, and his son Jotham had to take over the responsibilities of the throne (2 Chron. 26:16-23).

As in the case of Uzziah, the rejection of God's Word and His covenant comes with severe consequences, no matter who is guilty of the offence. Even though Judah is God's 'treasured possession,' He will send 'fire upon Judah and it will eat up the royal citadels of Jerusalem.' Nothing is more destructive than fire. It not only destroys, but it totally consumes such that little to nothing is salvageable when the smoke finally clears. Judah will experience the most devastating destruction known at that time. In 701 B.C., Sennacherib, the Assyrian king, marched against Judah and claimed to have laid siege and conquered forty-six cities and to have made King Hezekiah 'a prisoner in Jerusalem, his royal residence, like a bird in a cage. I surrounded him with earthwork in order to molest those who were leaving his city's gate.'[37] Amos' prophecy ultimately came true by means of the Babylonians under the leadership of King Nebuchadnezzar. Nebuchadnezzar invaded Judah and conquered Jerusalem three times in 605, 597, and 586 B.C. It was in 586 B.C. that he burnt down most of the city and destroyed the Temple.[38] At about that time, Ezekiel prophesied saying,

> Thus says the Lord GOD: This is Jerusalem. I have set her in the center of the nations, with countries all around her. And she

---
36. See Matthew 7:15-27.
37. Alfred J. Hoerth, *Archaeology and the Old Testament*, (Grand Rapids: Baker Books, 1998), 348-49.
38. See the book of Lamentations for Jeremiah's description of Jerusalem's fall.

has rebelled against my rules by doing wickedness more than the nations, and against my statutes more than the countries all around her; for they have rejected my rules and have not walked in my statutes. Therefore thus says the Lord God: Because you are more turbulent than the nations that are all around you, and have not walked in my statutes or obeyed my rules, and have not even acted according to the rules of the nations that are all around you, therefore thus says the Lord God: Behold, I, even I, am against you. And I will execute judgments in your midst in the sight of the nations. And because of all your abominations I will do with you what I have never yet done, and the like of which I will never do again (Ezek. 5:5-9).

Instead of being a light to nations showing forth the glory of God, Judah became an example to nations of what happens when God's people reject His covenant and are found unfaithful to their God.

Study Questions

1. What are some possible reasons why Amos proclaimed judgment upon foreign nations to an Israelite audience?

2. Why is disregard for human life so reprehensible to God?

3. How do people devalue others today?

4. What are ways people exploit others today?

5. Why is it important to God for people to keep their promises to others?

6. Why did Amos' declarations of judgment against the pagan nations omit any condemnation of their idolatry?

7. What effect might this message have had on Amos' audience with Judah as the seventh nation on his list?

3

The Wrong Way to Respond to God's Grace
(Amos 2:6-16)

My parents had only two children, both sons. My brother is the elder, and he is almost nine years older than me. I remember times when he might do something resulting in my parents' discipline. I would pay close attention to what he had done to get himself into trouble. My hope was to avoid the same outcome. I wanted to steer clear of making the same mistake. In many instances, I did learn from his mistakes, but I have to admit I had a knack of making many more of my own than my brother ever made. The point is we may sometimes learn from the mistakes of others. Hopefully, such is the case when we look at Israel's wayward response to the grace God had shown His people.

Amos' eighth and climactic indictment against the nations comes against Israel, the very audience to whom he has been preaching up to this point. Surely, Amos' Israelite audience was pleased to hear of God's judgments coming upon the other nations, all of which had troubled relations with Israel at one point or another. Moreover, they were probably pleased Judah was the seventh nation indicted, given the history of animosity between the two. Normally, the seventh nation would have been the last, since seven usually symbolizes completion and climax in the Scriptures. However, to Israel's surprise, Amos has an eighth nation on the list, and it is Israel. Thus, as the eighth nation on the list, Israel's transgressions exceed what one might expect.

Like Nathan with David (2 Sam. 12:1-13), Amos cleverly drew Israel into the center of his circle of judgment. If God was going to judge the other nations for their sins, then He also was going to judge Israel for its transgressions. As the Israelites were quick to applaud the Lord's condemnation of the nations, they were sealing their own fate. They were admitting that such sins deserved God's wrath. Imagine how the mood of the audience must have taken a serious one-hundred-eighty degree turn when Israel became the subject of God's condemnation. Amos unquestionably went from 'hero to zero' rather quickly. It is always easy to recognize and talk about the sins of others, but it is quite another thing when it comes to recognizing and talking about one's own failures. Amos' concern was for his obedience to God and the spiritual condition of God's people. He was not there to win a popularity contest or run for political office. Amos' concern for his people and his obedience to the Lord should be an example to all who are called to proclaim the Word of God, demonstrating how we should speak the truth in love. What was Amos' message to Israel?

They Chose to Follow in the Examples of Their Oppressors (2:6-8)
A number of years ago my son thought he had an extremely oppressive father because his father required him to do 'horrific' things such as clean his room, take out the garbage, and other menial chores. He looked at me and said, 'I cannot wait until I have children of my own.' I asked him, 'Why?' His response was, 'So that I can be as mean to them as you are being to me.' I thought he would not want to put his future children through the same 'cruel and unusual punishment' he was enduring. Nonetheless, it is amazing how many times the oppressed longs one day to be the oppressor rather than one who desires to do right when in a position of authority and power. Such seems to be the case with Israel. People who were once bullied by others have now become bullies themselves.

As with the other nations, Amos begins with the same pattern of 'three and for four' as he emphasizes the complete and ongoing nature of Israel's disobedience to God and that God's patience with them is now coming to an end. Its transgressions are directly related to the Lord's covenant with Israel. Nevertheless, it is not so much in the area one might expect. Amos has very little to say about Israel's worshiping other gods. His greatest concern is Israel's disregard for one another as God's people. A nation that has a long history of oppression at the hands of other nations has become entrenched in oppressive behavior toward its own people.

They were overcome with *greed*. The Israelites were guilty of selling into slavery those who have been falsely accused of owing money or they were selling into slavery those who could not pay off very small debts.[1] If the creditors would have given those in debt just a little more time, the debts could have been paid. In the first instance, the creditors would have been guilty of lying and stealing. In the second instance, the creditors would have been well within their rights to have brought those who defaulted on their debts to court, but to do so to otherwise innocent people was to disregard the very heart of the *tôrâ*. According to the Lord's instruction and stipulations, the wealthy had the responsibility of looking out for the poor by sharing with the needy. Instead of showing mercy in the matter of a trivial amount of debt that amounted to a small amount of silver or the cheap price of a pair of sandals, they enslaved a person, so making it almost impossible for the debt to be paid. In other words, they were selling people into slavery over nickels and dimes or over the price of a pair of flip-flops. This is the case where a person may be technically right but still be wrong. They were misusing the law for their own ends and oppressing their brothers along the way. Job lived a life in accordance with the spirit of God's law and expresses his understanding of righteous living when he says,

> If I have withheld anything that the poor desired, or have caused the eyes of the widow to fail, or have eaten my morsel alone, and the fatherless has not eaten of it (for from my youth the fatherless grew up with me as with a father, and from my mother's womb

---

1. See Exodus 21:2-11; Deuteronomy 15:12-18.

I guided the widow), if I have seen anyone perish for lack of clothing, or the needy without covering, if his body has not blessed me, and if he was not warmed with the fleece of my sheep, if I have raised my hand against the fatherless, because I saw my help in the gate, then let my shoulder blade fall from my shoulder, and let my arm be broken from its socket. For I was in terror of calamity from God, and I could not have faced his majesty (Job 31:16-23).[2]

Jesus explains the heart of God's law when he quotes Deuteronomy 6:5 and Leviticus 19:18:

You shall love the Lord your God with all your heart and with all your soul and with all your mind. This is the great and first commandment. And a second is like it: You shall love your neighbor as yourself. On these two commandments depend all the Law and the Prophets (Matt. 22:37-40)

And Paul says:

Bear one another's burdens, and so fulfil the law of Christ. Do not be deceived: God is not mocked, for whatever one sows, that will he also reap. For the one who sows to his own flesh will from the flesh reap corruption, but the one who sows to the Spirit will from the Spirit reap eternal life. And let us not grow weary of doing good, for in due season we will reap, if we do not give up. So then, as we have opportunity, let us do good to everyone, and especially to those who are of the household of faith (Gal. 6:2, 7-10).

While the creditors may have been technically right, they were completely wrong. They had missed the purpose of the *tôrâ*. They failed to love their neighbor as themselves, and failure to love one's neighbor is a failure to love God in truth.

Furthermore, the Israelites were guilty of *pride*, treating the poor like dirt upon which to trample. They had established a society that stamped upon the rights of the poor. They treated them with disdain and exploited them by perverting justice. The poor were robbed of what little they owned, they were robbed of justice, and they were robbed of their dignity. They were taken advantage of in every way. However, the behavior of the wealthy demonstrated their lack of godly wisdom. Proverbs 22:22 states: 'Do not rob the poor, because he is poor,

---

2. Honeycutt, 39.

or crush the afflicted at the gate, for the LORD will plead their cause and rob of life those who rob them.' The way people use their position of power and authority reveals much about their character (or lack thereof). Amos' indictment indicates the time of judgment has come.

However, Amos was not finished with his list of oppressions committed by Israel. They were guilty of *immorality*. He continues saying that a father and his son have sexual relations with a young female household employee.[3] It is the picture of a father and son taking advantage of an Israelite maiden who worked for their family, was in need of her job, and in a position to be taken advantage of. The message was clear: if she failed to cooperate with them in their sexual immorality and abuse, she would lose her job. The irony is that it was sexual perversion and promiscuity that had polluted the Promised Land before Israel entered it. Niehaus says:

> When the Lord reminded them, in Leviticus 18, that because of such sexual evils he was driving out the nations before them, he was not giving an idle reminder. He was making an important point: if they polluted themselves with such sin, as the Canaanites had done, he would drive them out of the land, just as he had driven out the Canaanites. God will not abide iniquity in the earth for long, nor among his people whom he has created to be children of light (Deut. 4:5-6; Rom. 13:12-14; Eph. 5:8-20).[4]

What is the result of these immoral and unethical actions of oppression against the weak and defenceless? The result is the Lord's name is profaned. Every act of oppression against another is ultimately the profanation of the Lord's name. It is profaned in Israel, and since Israel is the Lord's witness to the nations, his name also is profaned to the nations. The Lord is greatly concerned about His reputation. Instead of bringing honor to His name and showing the nations the greatness of its God, Israel has brought disrepute upon itself and the name of the Lord.

To make matters worse, they were guilty of *hypocrisy*. The upper class of Israel flaunted their sins before the Lord in their religious feasts that took place at their altars. First, Amos says

---

3. Gary V. Smith, *Amos* (Ross-shire, Great Britain: Mentor, 1998), 121-2.
4. Niehaus, 366.

the elite were using the coats they had taken from the poor who owed them money to lie on, as they went to worship the Lord. They were taking the only coats those people had into their religious festivals, even though the law prohibited one from keeping a coat that had been given in pledge after sunset (Exod. 22:26). The wealthy came to the Lord's altar desiring mercy when they had failed to show mercy themselves. It is difficult to imagine the poor had such nice cloaks that the wealthy would want to wear them in order to make a fashion statement. Perhaps they were showing off their latest conquests and status of power over the weak or maybe their own cloaks were too nice to put on the ground. Second, they brought wine to their feasts that they had purchased with the fines they had wrongfully collected from the poor. The elite and wealthy of Israel pandered to their own indulgences as they took the very coat off of a man's back and used his last few shekels to purchase fine wine for their times of worship. What irony!

They Had Forgotten the Example of the Lord (2:9-11)
Amos described what Israel has been doing, but now he turns to the Lord as his subject and reminds the Israelites of what the Lord has done. In contrast to Israel's infidelity to the covenant with the Lord and in contrast to its oppression of the poor and the weak, through Amos the Lord emphatically reminds Israel of His faithfulness to the covenant and His continued kindness to His people when they were poor and weak. He cared for them when no one else would. Notice how the Lord demonstrated His loving kindness to Israel:

(1) The Lord destroyed their enemies
'Amorites' refers to the entire population of Canaan when Joshua led Israel into Canaan.[5] The height of the Amorites is likened to cedars, trees often renowned for their great height in the Old Testament, and their strength is likened to that of the oak, which was known for its strength among trees.[6] When Israel's spies first saw the Canaanites, the spies thought

---

5. See Genesis 48:22; Joshua 24:15; Judges 6:10; 2 Samuel 21:2.
6. See Numbers 13:28; Deuteronomy 1:28; 2:10, 21; 9:2; Joshua 14:12, 15; 15:14; Isaiah 44:14; Ezekiel 27:5-6; Zechariah 11:1-2.

themselves to be like grasshoppers compared to the Canaanite giants (Num. 13:33). The Israelites claimed because the Lord hated them He brought them out of Egypt in order for the Amorites to destroy them (Deut. 1:27). Nonetheless, it was because the Lord had loved Israel that He brought them out of Egypt and destroyed the Amorites. The Lord is reminding the people that were it not for His going before Israel into battle as they entered the Promised Land, they would never have defeated the Amorites. The Israelites were herdsmen who had been wandering around in the wilderness for forty years prior to entering Canaan. They were not skilled, seasoned battle-hardened warriors. Their victory came only by their Divine Warrior, the Lord God (Exod. 23:20-23). How many times have we begun to doubt God's love for us when we encountered difficulties in life only to discover the Lord was with us all along and that He lovingly brought us through the difficulties to a better place, demonstrating to us His unfailing loving kindness for His children? How many times in the present do we forget what He has done in the past?

(2) The Lord completely removed the threat of their enemies
By the time Amos delivers his message, the Amorites have ceased to be a military threat to Israel or an obstacle to Israel's occupation of the land. Ultimately, the Lord had totally annihilated the Amorites. The destruction of 'his fruit above' and 'his roots beneath' poetically describes how the Lord ended the posterity of the Amorites. Because of their Divine Warrior, Israel would never again experience any more anxiety on account of the Amorites. The threat of the Amorite was no more. Likewise, it is because of our Divine Warrior that our enemy, death, is no more. By the cross and the resurrection, the Lord Jesus Christ has destroyed death, never more to be a threat to those who by faith have come to Him (1 Cor. 15:55-57). Apart from Christ's work all would be spiritually and eternally dead in sin.

(3) The Lord delivered them from slavery
As slaves in Egypt, the Israelites were mere property of their masters. They were put on the selling blocks alongside sheep and cattle. The Israelite males were worth between twenty

and thirty shekels when they were in Egypt.[7] Note Moses' description of Israel in Egypt:

> And he said to his people, 'Behold, the people of Israel are too many and too mighty for us. Come, let us deal shrewdly with them, lest they multiply, and, if war breaks out, they join our enemies and fight against us and escape from the land.' Therefore they set taskmasters over them to afflict them with heavy burdens. They built for Pharaoh store cities, Pithom and Raamses. But the more they were oppressed, the more they multiplied and the more they spread abroad. And the Egyptians were in dread of the people of Israel. So they ruthlessly made the people of Israel work as slaves and made their lives bitter with hard service, in mortar and brick, and in all kinds of work in the field. In all their work they ruthlessly made them work as slaves (Exod. 1:9-14).
>
> During those many days the king of Egypt died, and the people of Israel groaned because of their slavery and cried out for help. Their cry for rescue from slavery came up to God (Exod. 2:23).
>
> And the Egyptians treated us harshly and humiliated us and laid on us hard labor. Then we cried to the LORD, the God of our fathers, and the LORD heard our voice and saw our affliction, our toil, and our oppression (Deut. 26:6-7).

Israel was in bondage and sorely oppressed, yet the Lord heard its cry. He brought down one of the most powerful empires to exist up to that time and mercifully redeemed Israel, miraculously delivered them, and graciously brought them into a covenant relationship with Himself. God made Israel His treasured possession from among all the nations.[8] The same is true of believers today. We were once enslaved to sin, but the Lord has graciously called us to Himself and saved us. Paul writes to Titus, saying:

> For we ourselves were once foolish, disobedient, led astray, slaves to various passions and pleasures, passing our days in malice and envy, hated by others and hating one another. But when the goodness and loving kindness of God our Savior appeared, he saved us, not because of works done by us in righteousness, but according to his own mercy, by the washing of regeneration and

---

7. Kenneth A. Kitchen, *On the Reliability of the Old Testament* (Grand Rapids: Eerdmans Publishing Company, 2003), 344-5; also see Exodus 21:32.
8. See Exodus 19:5; Deuteronomy 7:6; 14:2; 26:18; Malachi 3:17.

renewal of the Holy Spirit, whom he poured out on us richly through Jesus Christ our Savior, so that being justified by his grace we might become heirs according to the hope of eternal life (Titus 3:3-7).

(4) The Lord led them to their destination with His providential care
In the wilderness, the Lord made His continual presence known to Israel every step of the way. He led them with a cloud by day and a pillar of fire by night (Exod. 13:21-22). The Levites carried His ark of the covenant before them as they traveled, and it rested in the tabernacle at the center of their encampments (Num. 10:33; 2:2; Exod. 40:21). He miraculously provided them with food and water (Exod. 16:13-16; 17:6; Neh. 9:20-21). He protected them from the dangers of the wilderness. The Lord graciously did all of these things so He might demonstrate His loving kindness to Israel and so that Israel might inherit the land of the Amorites. Those of us who are believers also experience the blessing and privilege of the Lord's presence and the indwelling of His Holy Spirit along with His provision for our daily needs.[9]

(5) The Lord gave them a land as their inheritance
For hundreds of years the Israelites had been enslaved in a foreign land, having no land of their own. Nevertheless, the Lord delivered them from their oppressors and brought them into a good land flowing with milk and honey as their inheritance from the Lord (Josh. 24:5-8). God was faithful to His promise to Abraham and their forefathers.[10] Those who are believers are also the offspring of Abraham and heirs of the promise to Abraham to be heirs of the world. As children of God we are fellow heirs with Christ (Gal. 3:29; Rom. 4:13; 8:16-17).

(6) The Lord gave them spiritual leaders
One of the greatest gifts God gave to Israel was spiritual leadership. The prophets were godly men who communicated God's message by their lives and actions, but their primary

---

9. See Matthew 6:25-34; 28:20; John 14:17; Romans 8:11; 1 Corinthians 3:16; 6:19; 2 Timothy 1:14; Hebrews 13:5.
10. See Genesis 12:7; 15:18-21; 17:8; 26:4; 28:4, 13-14; 35:12; 50:24; 1 Kings 4:21.

focus was on the verbal proclamation of God's Word to Israel. These messengers 'created a continual chain of constant communication between God and Israel. Amos is now the latest link in the prophetic continuum.'[11] The prophets served the purpose of fulfilling one of the roles pastors in the Church are called to fulfill today. The prophets communicated God's Word to God's people, teaching them, reproving them, correcting them, and training them in righteousness, so that the people of God might be competent and equipped for every good work (2 Tim. 3:16-17). Even their messages of judgment demonstrated God's mercy and grace as they served as warnings and opportunities for repentance and reconciliation to God (Jer. 18:7-8).

The Nazirites communicated a message of commitment to God, not so much by what they said but by how they lived. They followed a disciplined lifestyle in order to demonstrate their commitment to the Lord (Num. 6:1-20). Some became Nazirites as the result of a vow made by a parent such as Hannah made for Samuel (1 Sam. 1:11). In Samson's case, a messenger of the Lord visited Samson's barren mother, announced his birth, and told her Samson would be a Nazirite (Judg. 13:3-5). Still, it is possible others voluntarily took the vow to become Nazirites themselves, and they could last for a set period of time. When the period of the vow ended, the Nazirite cut off his hair and burned it, signifying the end of the vow.[12] The Nazirite vow carried with it some prohibitions. First, they abstained from anything that came from the vine, including alcohol; this distinction would have been quite apparent in their culture and a contrast to the practice of devotees to other gods and the drunken feasts that were part of their pagan cults. Second, just as distinctive was their prohibition to cut their hair. Their untrimmed hair served as a sign they completely belonged to God and was in contrast to the pagans who shaved their heads for their gods. Third, Nazirites avoided contact with the dead, symbolizing they served the one true living God and contrasting any pagan practices of necromancy. Fourth, the Nazirites abstained from

---

11. Paul, 92.
12. R. K. Harrison, 'Nazirite,' in *The International Standard Bible Encyclopedia*, ed. Geoffrey W. Bromiley, rev. ed. [ISBE] (Grand Rapids: Eerdmans, 1986), 501-2.

Amos 2:6-16

eating unclean food, demonstrating their consecration to the Lord (Judg. 13:7).

(7) The Lord gave them ample evidence of His kindness toward them
The Lord completes His list of examples of His loving kindness shown to Israel by asking the question, 'Is it not indeed so, O people of Israel?' In other words, Israel could not plead ignorance when it came to a history of God's dealings with His people. They knew what God had done for them, and they knew why. As a result, they were without excuse for their actions.

People Who Rebel Against God Will Oppose Those Who Live For God (2:12)
God gave the Nazirites to Israel in order that they would be 'spiritual billboards' reminding the people of Israel that the Lord was worthy of Israel's total devotion and faithfulness. They served as symbols of Israel's unique relationship to God among the nations—they were distinct, holy. Then again, to a people who were rebelling against God and who were unfaithful to their covenant with Him, the presence of the prophets and Nazirites was more of a bother than a blessing. Just like no one wants to hear how badly one may be hurting one's body as one sits down to eat a tantalizing hot fudge sundae, so the Israelites had no stomach for hearing the prophets point out Israel's rebellious ways. Likewise, few enjoy eating the tantalizing hot fudge sundae when someone sitting across from them is eating a healthy fruit salad. Just the presence of the Nazirites became annoying to the Israelites as they witnessed the contrast of their respective lifestyles. If misery loves company, so do sinners. Sinners hate being reminded of what they are whether by word or deed.

Consequently, the Israelites sought to eliminate their nuisance. First, they corrupted the Nazirites by coercing them to drink wine and thus break their vows. Those in rebellion against God rejoice when one who has been faithful to God falls. It makes the rebellious ones feel better about themselves as the once-strong message of righteousness is rendered impotent. No longer do they have to face the accusation of a pure and devoted life in their midst. Furthermore, the Israelites opposed God's prophets. Throughout Israel's history of unfaithfulness to the Lord there are many instances where the Israelites attempted to silence God's messengers.[13] Even Amos faces such opposition when Amaziah the priest insisted that Amos go back home to Judah and prophesy there instead of in Israel (7:12-13). The Israelites were glad to hear Amos condemn their neighbors, but when he turned the spotlight of God's judgment upon them, they had heard enough.

With so much conflict in very many churches today, it would be good for us to ask where we stand. Most believers tend to think of the oppression that comes from being a child of God, and many of us tend to believe that if we are in the midst of conflict we are the ones being wronged. We are the oppressed. Yet how many of us take a good look at ourselves and instead of defending our actions put our attitudes and actions under the light of God's Word? Could it be we are guilty of being oppressors ourselves? We ask the Lord to change the hearts of others, but do we ask the Lord to change our own hearts? As it was with the Israelites, the way we conduct ourselves may be right in our own eyes, but is it right in God's eyes? Are we prayerfully, actively supporting the godly leaders God has sent us, or are we opposing them and the work God has sent them to do? Do we encourage them to proclaim the whole counsel of God's Word and follow the leadership of the Holy Spirit or do we muzzle our leaders or coerce them to do things our way with threats of opposition or withheld support?

Our Failure to Show Kindness to Others Forfeits God's Kindness To Us (2:13)

The Lord had graciously saved and protected Israel from its oppressors in great and miraculous ways on numerous occasions. Such kindness bestowed upon Israel should have motivated them to show similar kindness to others. God called His people into a covenant relationship with Himself so that they might reflect His glory and character to one another and to the nations. Instead, Israel became like the very people from whom God had rescued them. All of God's children are responsible to respond to His grace in a way that reflects His

---

13. See 1 Kings 13:4; 18:4; 19:2, 10; 22:26-27; 2 Kings 6:31; Isaiah 30:10; Jeremiah 2:30; 11:21; 18:18; 20:10; 26:23.

character and glory. The Lord Jesus Christ teaches this truth in Matthew 18:23-34:

> Therefore the kingdom of heaven may be compared to a king who wished to settle accounts with his servants. When he began to settle, one was brought to him who owed him ten thousand talents. And since he could not pay, his master ordered him to be sold, with his wife and children and all that he had, and payment to be made. So the servant fell on his knees, imploring him, 'Have patience with me, and I will pay you everything.' And out of pity for him, the master of that servant released him and forgave him the debt. But when that same servant went out, he found one of his fellow servants who owed him a hundred denarii, and seizing him, he began to choke him, saying, 'Pay what you owe.' So his fellow servant fell down and pleaded with him, 'Have patience with me, and I will pay you.' He refused and went and put him in prison until he should pay the debt. When his fellow servants saw what had taken place, they were greatly distressed, and they went and reported to their master all that had taken place. Then his master summoned him and said to him, 'You wicked servant! I forgave you all that debt because you pleaded with me. And should not you have had mercy on your fellow servant, as I had mercy on you?' And in anger his master delivered him to the jailers, until he should pay all his debt.

Instead of learning from the Lord's gracious example, Israel chose to follow the ways of the Amorites. In these verses from Amos' message, the Lord uses the emphatic personal pronoun to communicate what He had done and is about to do. He says, 'I destroyed,' 'I brought you up,' and now 'I will press you down.' In fact, the text is doubly emphatic as He repeats the word 'I' three times in the Hebrew text. Just as the wealthy and powerful pressed down the poor and weak, the Lord will press down upon Israel. The weight of the judgment will be such that Israel will be crushed under its weight like a wagon under too heavy a load. Note the irony. They will have so much ill-gotten abundance and prosperity that the cart will break under it.[14] That which was the focus of their sin will become their undoing. Israel's prosperity will certainly draw the attention of other nations that covet what Israel has.

---

14. Paul, 95.

God often uses what has been the object of one's sin as His instrument of judgment.

God Opposes Oppressors No Matter Who They Are (2:14-16)

Amos' description of the destruction of Israel's army must have been unbelievable to his audience. With the exception of Israel's days of glory under the reigns of David and Solomon, at no other time in history did Israel amass so great an army as they had during the reign of Jeroboam II.[15] Even so, Amos' portrayal is one of total annihilation of Israel's military. Regardless of how invincible one might believe oneself to be, God will oppose the oppressor of the poor and powerless. Furthermore, regardless of one's standing before God, whether pagans or His children, He will not allow such sin to go unpunished. The Lord will always stand up to bullies.

Amos' depiction of Israel's fall reveals a keen sense of knowledge of warfare in his day. Every ability and tool of war will fail. Swiftness is the first attribute one would develop for battle. Why? Because no matter how large or strong one's opponent, the first to strike is often the victor. Swiftness provides the first advantage in combat, but what if a warrior's opponent is equally fast? If his enemy is equally as quick as he, then the warrior's next resource is his strength to overpower his enemy. But what if the enemy matches both the warrior's swiftness and strength, then the key to victory rests upon the warrior's keen sense of prowess and skill to defeat his adversary. Amos' message is clear. These three foundations of close combat and military maneuvering will fail when Israel's time comes.

Notice how Amos' depiction of Israel's downfall follows the typical progression of battle in his day. When an enemy approached, it was the archers with their long-ranged missiles that commenced the defense of an army as the enemy approached. Next, the infantry would engage the attackers. Finally, the commander would utilize his swift cavalry to take advantage of the exposed weaknesses in the enemy's formations as the confusion and fog of battle began to sweep

---

15. See the introductory comments for Amos 1:1-2, and also see Amos 6:13.

Amos 2:6-16

over the battlefield. The cavalry could effectively deliver a crushing blow leading to victory.

Like so many battles before, Israel's military will attempt to defeat its enemy in this way. However, in the battle Amos describes, the archers, the infantry, and the cavalry will all attempt to flee. Like the Union soldiers who fled back across the Potomac River to safety out of the Shenandoah Valley from Stonewall Jackson's foot cavalry, Amos predicts a 'Great Skedaddle.'[16] Only in Israel's instance, none will escape. As the number seven often symbolizes completeness in the Scriptures, Amos employs seven various descriptive aspects of the battle in order to portray the complete obliteration of Israel's military machine.

Does such a judgment indicate God is finished with Israel? Certainly, Israel's breaking of the covenant means God is in no way obligated by Israel to keep the covenant. Nonetheless, God is obligated to Himself and His own faithfulness in spite of Israel's continued unfaithfulness. So how might one understand this Word of judgment? First, it should be understood as God's unfailing grace in the face of such blatant disobedience. God had warned Israel through Moses of the consequences of their unfaithfulness to the Lord and their neglect of those in need. Yet once again through His prophet he warns them, giving them the opportunity to repent. Second, God's judgment is a time of purging of those who are only posing to be children of God, and it is a time of purifying for those who truly are children of God.[17] Just because people were descendants of Abraham did not mean they were children of God. Not everyone of Abraham is of Abraham (John 8:39; Rom. 9:7). It would do people in the Church today well to remember this truth. Just because we belong to a local church or have participated in religious activities does not necessarily make us children of God. We are saved by grace through faith in the Lord Jesus Christ (Eph. 2:8-9). However, we are saved for the purpose of doing good works in order to reflect the glory of God and testify to the salvation that comes only through His Son. A call to a covenant relationship with

---

16. A term the Confederates often used to describe Union 'retreats' or better describes routes during the American Civil War.
17. Motyer, 64.

God through His Son, Jesus Christ, is a call to walk in a manner worthy of such a calling (Eph. 2:10; 3:10–4:3). Third, while God's children will always be His children, our sin results in God's displeasure and our loss of blessing. The teenager who breaks curfew, continues to be the son of his father, but there are both relational and practical consequences from his rebellion against his father. Only when confession and repentance happen can there truly be forgiveness and reconciliation.

STUDY QUESTIONS

1. What possible significance is there in the fact Israel was Amos' eighth nation to confront?
2. How much are people influenced by negative examples from their past?
3. Like the people of Israel, are there instances today where one might technically be right and yet be wrong in God's eyes?
4. How does Amos characterize Israel's sin?
5. How does the sin of God's people reflect upon God's reputation?
6. How does the Lord demonstrate His loving kindness to His people?
7. Why do the ungodly seek to silence the testimony of the godly?

4

The Privilege of Responsibility
(Amos 3:1-15)

I once heard a gentleman discussing life in prison. He said that the true indicator of freedom in society is having responsibilities, and the mark of imprisonment is the loss of responsibilities. Most inmates have lost the privilege of having responsibilities in their lives. Someone else does almost everything for them. Someone else determines where they will live. Someone else chooses what clothes they will wear. Someone else chooses what times they will get up in the morning and go to bed at night. In fact, someone else chooses what their schedule will be for an entire day. Someone else ensures what they will eat and what will be on the menu. Most inmates have one primary responsibility, to do what they are told to do. Even if the inmates choose to resist this responsibility, someone else will determine the consequences for their actions. Inmates have little to no privacy because they have shown themselves irresponsible. We often think of responsibility as a negative thing, a weight bearing down upon us. Many might believe that true freedom would be the absence of responsibility. Obviously, everyone needs times of rest in order to recharge oneself so that one may continue carrying out one's responsibilities. However, those who have lost their freedom can tell us the loss of having responsibilities truly is a punishment, not a blessing.[1] The privilege of freedom brings with it the privilege of responsibility.

---

1. For an intriguing and graphic look at life in prison from the perspective of an inmate, see K. C. Carceral, *Behind A Convict's Eyes: Doing Time in a Modern Prison* (Florence, KY: Wadsworth Publishing, 2003).

Chapter 3 of Amos begins a new section of the book where Amos brings a series of three messages introduced by the words, 'Hear this word' (3:1; 4:1; 5:1). Verses 1-2 not only reiterate what Amos has just indicated concerning God's judgment coming upon Israel, these verses also lay the foundation for the remainder of Amos' message concerning Israel. Why does the Lord target Israel in such a scrupulous way? It is because of the privileges God has given to them. God's people sometimes have difficulty handling the privileges they have in Christ. Either they begin to think God has shown them special favor over other believers or they tend to conclude they must be better than others.[2] Both conclusions fail to recognize God's blessings come by God's grace and by no merit of their own. As Amos addresses his audience, he makes it clear that along with the many privileges God's people enjoy comes the privilege of responsibility.

God has distinctively blessed His people with privileges (3:1-2a)

The Lord blessed Israel with a number of privileges. First, God has uniquely blessed them in the past with His Word, just as He is blessing them once again through Amos (3:1). Scripture attests to how God uniquely blessed Israel with His Word:

> He said, 'The LORD came from Sinai and dawned from Seir upon us; he shone forth from Mount Paran; he came from the ten thousands of holy ones, with flaming fire at his right hand. Yes, he loved his people, all his holy ones were in his hand; so they followed in your steps, receiving direction from you, when Moses commanded us a law, as a possession for the assembly of Jacob (Deut. 33:2-4).

> He established a testimony in Jacob and appointed a law in Israel, which he commanded our fathers to teach to their children (Ps. 78:5).

> To begin with, the Jews were entrusted with the oracles of God (Rom. 3:2).

> Long ago, at many times and in many ways, God spoke to our fathers by the prophets (Heb. 1:1).

---

2. Honeycutt, 52.

Israel was the first nation to hear God's Word, and it was the only nation to receive God's Word directly from God's messengers. Israel was privileged above all other nations because God revealed Himself to Israel in a way that no other nation experienced.

Today, it is a great privilege for God's people to have His written Word. God's Word reveals so much to us. It reveals who Jesus is. He is the creator. He is the way, the truth, and the life. He is the bread of life. He is the living water. He is the mighty judge, and He is the Savior. He is the Lord. The greatest blessing of having God's written Word is that through the Holy Spirit it reveals to us the Living Word, our Lord and Savior Jesus Christ (John 1:1-14). As God spoke to Israel by the prophets He has spoken to His Church 'by his Son' (Heb. 1:2). Furthermore, God's Word reveals who we are. We are created in His image. We are sinners by nature and by choice. We can be saved from sin and death by grace through faith in the Lord Jesus Christ. We were created to worship God and bring glory to Him. We are to be witnesses to His salvation.

Second, the Lord established Israel as a people. Jacob went down into Egypt a 'wandering Aramean' with 'few in number', and 'became a nation, great, mighty, and populous' (Deut. 26:5). The Lord promised the patriarchs that he would make them a great nation, and He did.[3] Those who have trusted in Jesus Christ for their salvation have become part of the kingdom of God, with the Lord as their king. Paul says that the Lord 'has delivered us from the domain of darkness and transferred us to the kingdom of his beloved Son, in whom we have redemption, the forgiveness of sins' (Col. 1:13-14).[4]

Third, the Lord had delivered Israel from bondage. However, the Israelites appeared to view the Exodus from Egypt as a guarantee that the Lord would deliver His people out of every situation.[5] Therefore, they could do whatever they pleased because the Lord would save them. They failed to realize that

---

3. Genesis 15:5; 22:17; Exodus 32:13; Deuteronomy 10:22.
4. 1 Thessalonians 2:12; 2 Timothy 4:18; Hebrews 1:8; 12:28; James 2:5; 2 Peter 1:11.
5. Y. Hoffman, *The Doctrine of Exodus in the Bible* (Tel Aviv: Tel Aviv University, 1983), 35.

the Exodus should have reminded them of their privileged relationship with the Lord. With the privilege of freedom comes the privilege of responsibility. Israel treated the Exodus like a lucky rabbit's foot that would bring them God's favor in times of trouble, no matter what. They saw God's salvation as a safeguard from the consequences of their disobedience. God's grace is not to be taken in such a way that we think, 'If we sin more, God is given the opportunity to demonstrate more of His grace.' God's grace should motivate us to live righteously before God, especially when we consider the price God paid in order to show us such grace by the shedding of Christ's blood on the cross.

Fourth, of all the nations of the world, only Israel was God's elect. The Hebrew word translated 'known' signifies intimacy and a 'relationship in its fullest sense.'[6] Sometimes it has the meaning 'to select, to choose.'[7] The word may also be understood in the context of an ancient Near Eastern suzerain-vassal treaty where it has the legal meaning 'to recognize as a legitimate suzerain or vassal and to recognize treaty stipulations as binding.'[8] In this instance, the Lord is saying that Israel alone is His legitimate covenant partner—no one else. He has permanently bound Himself to Israel. The strongest language possible portrays God's covenant with His people. What greater privilege could any nation or person have than for the Lord to commit Himself to them in such a way?

Why did the Lord so commit Himself? First, it is because He loved Israel (Deut. 4:37). His love was not based upon any merit in them; instead it was based upon His heart. Second, the Lord chose Israel to be a kingdom of priests and a holy nation. It was through Israel that the nations would be blessed. It is for this reason the Lord promised to set Israel 'in praise and in fame and in honor high above all nations that he has made' (Deut. 26:19). The Lord gave Israel the greatest privilege given to any people when He made her His treasured possession out of all the families on the earth. Nevertheless, when God chose

---

6. Terence E. Fritheim, 'ידע' in *New International Dictionary of Old Testament Theology & Exegesis*, ed. Willem A. VanGemeren (Grand Rapids: Zondervan Publishing House, 1997), 2:411.

7. Paul, 101; see Genesis 18:19; Exodus 33:12, 17; Deuteronomy 9:24; Jeremiah 1:5; Hosea 13:5.

8. Ibid., 102.

Israel, He also gave them the privilege of having the greatest responsibility known to any people, to be His instrument of blessing to all nations. God's commitment to Israel was equalled by His commitment to His purpose for Israel. How was Israel to fulfill this purpose? Moses made it clear with a question: 'And now, Israel, what does the LORD your God require of you, but to fear the LORD your God, to walk in all his ways, to love him, to serve the LORD your God with all your heart and with all your soul, and to keep the commandments and statutes of the LORD, which I am commanding you today for your good?' (Deut. 10:12-13).

With the privilege of great responsibility comes a great accountability (3:2b)

Upon hearing Amos speak of all the privileges God had bestowed upon them, the Israelites probably were confident God would continue to bless them no matter what they did. After all, God had chosen Israel out of all the families of the earth to be His chosen people, His treasured possession. Imagine their shock, as Amos once again continued His message by stating the unexpected. Rather than saying what the people expected or wanted to hear, Amos told them that with great privilege comes the greater privilege of responsibility. They failed to realize that the greatest privilege is to serve the Lord as an instrument for His glory and purposes. Israel's disregard for their responsibility meant God would hold them accountable for their irresponsibility.

God's people were accountable to God for sinning *against themselves*. They had been so entrenched in their greed, pride, immorality, and religious hypocrisy that they had deceived themselves by assuming they could carry on in their lifestyle with impunity. They chose to recall the promises of blessing in the covenant, yet they ignored its warnings for disobedience. It resembles a type of preaching we might witness today where preachers only want to focus on what is positive. Their messages fail to address sin and its consequences. Some preach in such a manner in order to tell people what they want to hear, as opposed to what they need to hear, for the purpose of being popular. Still others probably tend to avoid speaking of sin and its consequences as a response to cold, harsh, legalistic preaching devoid of any message of hope or grace. Such preaching has done a great deal of damage to the Church. Nevertheless, just as it is wise for one to pay attention to the warning label on a bottle containing a toxic substance, it is wise for one to heed the warnings in God's Word. Negligence in this area is fatal, as Israel discovered.

God's people were accountable to God for sinning *against their own kinsmen*. While some of the laws in the *tôrâ* addressed the Israelites' relationships with foreigners, the vast majority of them either pertain to their relationship with God or with one another. Those who had been victimized by foreigners had become the oppressors of their own people. The Word of God clearly instructs God's people to do good to others, especially to those who are our brothers and sisters in the faith. People who are the recipients of God's kindness are to show kindness to others. This expectation was a substantial requirement of the covenant. It is interesting to note how in the Ten Commandments the first three commandments address Israel's relationship to God. The fourth serves as a transitional commandment as it addresses Israel's relationship to God and to others. Then the next six commandments address Israel's behavior to one another. The majority of the Ten Commandments focus on how people treat one another. Of course, all of the commandments are connected by the truth that one's love for others really reflects our love and devotion to God.

God's people were accountable also to God for their sinning *against the nations*. As God's chosen people, His only people out of all the families of the earth, God's reputation among the nations was closely identified with Israel's conduct and reputation. If the Lord would allow Israel to continue in its wicked ways it would communicate that either God approved of such conduct or He was powerless to do anything about it. Their behavior brought reproach upon the Lord's name by undermining His reputation as an omnipotent God of moral character. Israel's rebellious ways painted a false picture of the one true God. However, the Lord was so committed to His covenant with Israel and to using His people as an instrument of blessing in His mission of the redemption of the nations, that He forbade Israel to continue displaying a false representation of Him to these nations. God's discipline of His children was a corrective to their thinking and behavior, but also it was a corrective to the false image of God their misbehavior had communicated to others. His discipline of His children not only demonstrated His love for His own people but also His love for the world.

Ultimately, God's people were accountable to God because their sin was *against Him*. God had graciously blessed them, chosen them, and committed Himself to them in a way unknown to any other people. His loving kindness should have humbled Israel and stirred within the people a deep devotion and loyalty to God with a desire to keep His covenant. Their disregard and oppression of others demonstrated a disregard and contempt for God. As Jesus said:

> When the Son of Man comes in his glory, and all the angels with him, then he will sit on his glorious throne. Before him will be gathered all the nations, and he will separate people one from another as a shepherd separates the sheep from the goats. And he will place the sheep on his right, but the goats on the left. Then the King will say to those on his right, 'Come, you who are blessed by my Father, inherit the kingdom prepared for you from the foundation of the world. For I was hungry and you gave me food, I was thirsty and you gave me drink, I was a stranger and you welcomed me, I was naked and you clothed me, I was sick and you visited me, I was in prison and you came to me.' Then the righteous will answer him, saying, 'Lord, when did we see you hungry and feed you, or thirsty and give you drink? And when did we see you a stranger and welcome you, or naked and clothe you? And when did we see you sick or in prison and visit you?' And the King will answer them, 'Truly, I say to you, as you did it to one of the least of these my brothers, you did it to me.' Then he will say to those on his left, 'Depart from me, you cursed, into the eternal fire prepared for the devil and his angels. For I was hungry and you gave me no food, I was thirsty and you gave me no drink, I was a stranger and you did not welcome me, naked and you did not clothe me, sick and in prison and you did not visit me.' Then they also will answer, saying, 'Lord, when did we see you hungry or thirsty or a stranger or naked or sick or in prison, and did not minister to you?' Then he will answer them, saying, 'Truly, I say to you, as you did not do it to one of the least of these, you did not do it to me.' And these will go away into eternal punishment, but the righteous into eternal life' (Matt. 25:31-46).

The actions of God's people toward others are a reflection of their love or lack thereof for the Lord.

The Lord Jesus also said, 'Everyone to whom much was given, of him much will be required, and from him to whom they entrusted much, they will demand the more' (Luke 12:48b). Amos reminded Israel of the 'much' God had given His people. It was because of the 'much' God had given them that He demanded more from them. Notwithstanding, Israel rejected God's invitation to faithfulness and intimacy with Him, and instead chose a life of rebellion and self-centeredness (Deut. 6:5, 13; 10:12, 20; 11:1, 13). Therefore, faithful to His covenant, God would visit His judgment upon Israel (Deut. 27–28). A loving God is as faithful to discipline His children for their disobedience as He is to bless them in their obedience. Israel's privileges would fail to shield the people from God's discipline. In fact, the enormity of their privileges would be matched by the severity of God's judgment. Their rejection of God's unique love for Israel brought upon the nation tougher consequences than any other nation would experience. How so? On top of the physical suffering and losses the judgment would bring, they have lost fellowship with their Lord who had saved them and called them unto Himself. The price of sin is high indeed. Would that God's people would repent and experience the joy of forgiveness and reconciliation to God!

Remember the principle of cause and effect (3:3-6)
Actions result in consequences. The Lord has instilled this principle in His creation. Paul attests to this principle when he writes: 'Do not be deceived: God is not mocked, for whatever one sows, that will he also reap. For the one who sows to his own flesh will from the flesh reap corruption, but the one who sows to the Spirit will from the Spirit reap eternal life. And let us not grow weary of doing good, for in due season we will reap, if we do not give up' (Gal. 6:7-9). Newton's Third Law of Motion affirms this observation stating, 'For every action, there is an equal and opposite reaction.' It is the principle of cause and effect that Amos now addresses as he confronts Israel. He does so in an interesting way. Having delineated the privileges God had bestowed upon Israel and having

Amos 3:1-15

pronounced God's judgment upon Israel for its irresponsible response, in a Socratic-like fashion Amos raises a series of questions with obvious answers in order to drive home the point of his message.

In verse 3, his first question establishes a cause-and-effect relationship between two people. When do two people walk even a short distance side by side without both agreeing to do so? We would think it very strange if we were taking a walk by ourselves and a stranger was to come along and began to walk right next to us. Two individuals walk together because they have both agreed to do so. The effect is the two walking together as a result of the cause, their decision to walk together. Now it appears Israel has decided to walk alone.

Amos' second and third questions in verse 4 turn attention to the hunting practices of a lion. Normally, a lion roars either to communicate with other lions or to intimidate or warn other animals they are getting too close to danger. Sometimes they roar in frustration when their prey has spotted them and is able to get away. So does a lion roar when it is in hiding, attempting to catch its prey? Absolutely not. If it did, it would go hungry. Therefore, when a person hears the roar of a lion, it is probably a roar of warning (1:2; 3:8). Like a lion roaring when another has transgressed his boundaries, so the Lord roars from Zion warning Israel that it has transgressed upon His holy standards for His people. However, when God's judgment actually comes, the hungry Lion will strike so suddenly that the prey will only realize what has happened to it when it is too late to flee.

Amos' fourth and fifth questions in verse 5 address the nature of traps. Would a bird get caught in a trap on the ground if it were not baited to do so? Does a trap shut when nothing has sprung it? The answers are 'no.' Maybe the Israelites were counting on God to do for them what He had done in the past for David. David said, 'Blessed be the LORD, who has not given us as prey to their teeth! We have escaped like a bird from the snare of the fowlers; the snare is broken, and we have escaped! Our help is in the name of the LORD, who made heaven and earth' (Ps. 124:6-8). If they were expecting God to do the same for them, the people were sadly mistaken. This time there would be no escape or deliverance for Israel. How could people who continued in sin expect God to deliver them from the consequences of sin? Israel should not, and neither should we.

Amos' sixth question in verse 6 has an obvious answer too. Who would not be frightened to hear the watchman's sound of the trumpet as he alerts the city of an enemy army's approach? It must have been an ominous sound. Most of the time, sieges upon cities ended in the city's defeat. In those instances where a city withstood a siege, the inhabitants' survival came with a terrible cost of deprivation and death. The foreboding blast of the watchmen's trumpet signaled impending distress and extreme devastation. Amos' message is such a warning.

The seventh and presumed climactic question reveals who is the cause of any calamity that besets a city. It is the Lord God. Through His prophet Isaiah the Lord says, 'I form light and create darkness, I make well-being and create calamity, I am the LORD, who does all these things' (Isa. 45:7). Therefore, when Israel's day of calamity strikes, she must realize the Lord God is responsible for her calamity. Israel must recognize that the means God uses to bring about its judgment day is only His tool. He is responsible, and no one else is. The Assyrians may attack Israel, but they will be the instruments of God's wrath upon His people.

In His mercy, God warns His children of His imminent discipline (3:7-8)
Being a just God, the Lord pronounced His judgment on Israel because of its iniquities, yet in His mercy the Lord sent Amos to warn the people of their approaching doom. As a lion warns his adversaries of danger, so the Lord has roared so that Israel might fear Him and repent. The Lord never brings down His judgment upon His people without first sending them a word of warning. Why? It is because judgment is not God's 'default setting' when it comes to humanity. God's desire is for people to repent rather than perish (2 Pet. 3:9). James says, 'Mercy triumphs over judgment' (James 2:13). As unfaithful and disobedient to the Lord as Israel has been, God still warns His people so that they might have one more opportunity to repent and experience His forgiveness and reconciliation. The sometimes harsh words of Amos are God's words of tough love for His people. Israel has become so steeped in the mire of

Amos 3:1-15

their sin that they require a strong message. Amos spoke God's truth in love (Eph. 4:15). How much has our desire to avoid offending others diminished our willingness to speak the truth in love today?

Those who experience God's judgment deserve it (3:9-10)
As the Righteous Judge of All Creation sits in judgment upon Israel, Amos, His prosecutor, calls forth witnesses. His witnesses might be surprising. Amos calls forth the Philistines of Ashdod and the Egyptians. First, Amos calls them to witness the sinful activities of Israel's powerful and wealthy. No one could serve as better expert witnesses to oppression than the Philistines and the Egyptians who had a history of oppressing Israel. Their expertise as oppressors made them well suited to identify Israel as a fellow persecutor of the poor and weak. In other words, 'It takes one to know one.' Amos instructs them to gather on the mountains surrounding the city of Samaria, Israel's capital, and to witness all that is happening in the city. The Philistines and Egyptians would have a great view since the mountains surrounding the city are of higher elevation than that of the mountain upon which the city was located.

What is Amos calling the witnesses to see? He calls them to witness how Israel's rebellion against the Lord has brought about confusion and unrest. The nation is so entrenched in sin that Israel is incapable of doing right. The people lack integrity. They are hoarding all they have plundered from the victims of their crimes of personal violence and property theft. Even pagan nations like Philistia and Egypt can recognize how deserving of God's judgment Israel has become since the wickedness of Israel has surpassed the sins of the other nations.

Those who experience God's judgment will lose their sources of security (3:11-15)

(1) Their fortified ramparts (3:11-12)
A significant source of pride for Israel's rich and powerful was the nation's military and fortifications. Therefore, they believed their possessions were secure. However, just as the wealthy stole what little the poor had for sustenance, so an enemy will come to ransack and pillage the mighty fortifications of Israel's

rich and powerful. The might and power of their army and fortresses will be unable to withstand the onslaught. Those who have been the plunderers will become the plundered. How amazing it is that God's judgment targets the very seat of one's sin. When the prophet Elijah confronted Ahab for Israel's worship of Baal, he said there would be no rain until word was given for it to rain again. Baal, the storm god, could not make it rain when the one true and living God said there would be no rain. God's judgment is not random but pointed and reasoned.

Amos utilized a well-known law among herdsmen to describe what will become of Israel. If a shepherd could produce evidence that an animal under his care was torn by savage beasts and not lost as a result of negligence, then the evidence would absolve the shepherd of financial responsibility for the loss. The law stated that sufficient evidence would be some scrap of the animal's carcass (Exod. 22:12-13; see Gen. 31:39). Amos was saying that after Israel's judgment is complete, little of its former self will be remaining. Also, just as the shepherd was absolved of any responsibility for the animal attacked by some wild beast, so the Lord will be absolved of any judicial responsibility for what will happen to Israel.

(2) Their false religion (3:13-14)
Amos says when all the evidence comes to light, God will destroy the altars of Bethel, one of Israel's prominent religious shrines. Bethel is located about ten miles north of Jerusalem. It was one of two locations where Jeroboam built altars when he became the first king of the northern kingdom, Israel. Dan was the location of the other altar. Jeroboam established a religious cult to replace worship in Jerusalem by appointing its own priesthood with its own altars, accompanied by golden calves (1 Kings 12:28-33; 13:1-2). These altars served a dual purpose: they were the place where blood-sacrifices took place for the expiation of sin, and they were places of asylum—those who grasped the horns of the altar were immune from punishment.[9] The destruction of Bethel's altars signified the end of Israel's opportunity to make amends for sin and the end of her immunity from punishment.[10]

---
9. See Leviticus 16:18; Exodus 21:13-14; 1 Kings 1:50; 2:28.
10. Paul, 124.

Amos 3:1-15

(3) Their fancy residences (3:15)
The rich and powerful of Israel were so wealthy that many of them owned two luxurious homes symbolizing their status: one for the summer and one for the winter.[11] These immaculate houses were adorned with ivory and the finest decor their shekels could buy. Amos declares these great estates will come to nothing. The Lord will strike them down. What were once symbols of Israel's prosperity and financial security will become reminders of God's judgment upon those who oppress the poor and weak.

Is there any hope for Israel?
Amos' sermon appears devoid of any hope. However, there is hope. First, he indicates that, like the pieces of the animal left for the shepherd, there will be a remnant of Israel that will survive. Israel's judgment will be devastating, but it will not be a total annihilation of God's people. God will not abandon His purposes for Israel. Second, Amos' message provided hope to the oppressed. There is a time approaching when the Lord will avenge them, and their oppressors will be no more. God's judgment on some will be a blessing to others. Soon there will be an end to their suffering.

STUDY QUESTIONS

1. How is it a privilege for God's people to be given responsibilities by God?

2. How are God's people a privileged people?

3. For what were the Israelites accountable to God?

4. What is the principle of cause and effect?

5. How is a message of judgment merciful?

6. What were Israel's sources of security?

7. How significant is it that God will ultimately avenge His people?

---

11. Archeologists have discovered Herod's winter palace near Jericho. Having a winter home and a summer home was a status symbol in the ancient Near East.

5

Expressions of Self-centeredness
(Amos 4:1-13)

The Dutch poet, Piet Hein, wrote, 'People are self-centered to a nauseous degree. They will keep on about themselves while I'm explaining me.' If we were honest, most of us would have to agree that we are more self-centered than we would care to admit. Yet, there are few traits any more ungodly than self-centeredness. In Amos 4:1-13, Amos confronts Israel with her self-centeredness.

Self-centeredness expresses itself by self-absorption (4:1-3)
When I was a boy and first heard Amos' words, 'Hear this word, you cows of Bashan,' I was shocked that a preacher would call the women in his audience 'cows.' I wondered what would happen in the church where I was a member if the pastor called the women 'cows,' and I have to admit that I thought it might be interesting to find out. However, Amos' calling the wealthy women of Samaria 'cows' meant something different than it would probably mean today. The region that was called Bashan during the time of Amos is located east of the Sea of Galilee, measuring about 37 miles east to Mt Bashan, which is on the edge of the Arabian Desert. Bashan runs from north to south about 56 miles from Mt Hermon in the north to just south of the Yarmuk River.[1] Baly

---

1. Carl G. Rasmussen, *Zondervan NIV Atlas of the Bible* (Grand Rapids: Zondervan Publishing House, 1989), 29.

describes the region as 'wide open plains between 1600 and 2300 feet in height, and magnificently fertile.'[2] The western half of the region is exceptionally productive, with its volcanic soil combined with approximately 40 inches of rain each year.[3] During biblical times, Bashan served as a 'breadbasket' for Israel, with wheat as its primary crop. The region provided high-quality pastures for livestock: note the 'bulls of Bashan' (Ps. 22:12) and the 'fat beasts of Bashan' including rams, lambs, goats, and bulls (Ezek. 39:18).[4]

Given the agrarian culture of Israel and instances where comparisons to the best qualities of livestock and produce appear as positive expressions, the expression 'cows of Bashan' should probably be understood as an expression pertaining to luxury and privileged circumstances and not a negative reference to the women's weight or actual appearance.[5] In our vernacular, the term might be better understood as Amos addressing the 'stars' or 'divas of Samaria' or 'The Real Housewives of Samaria.'[6] These expressions probably communicate the picture Amos is portraying. Furthermore, in many cultures where the majority of the people have very little, being overweight is a sign of affluence and desirable. What is negative about Amos' use of the term probably has more to do with *how* they became 'cows of Bashan' rather than with the expression itself.

The women Amos is addressing are self-centered. Their main concern in life is self-indulgence, no matter whom it hurts in the process. Their sense of entitlement means no whim of theirs goes unmet as others suffer in order to make it happen. It is a picture of extortion, exploitation, and manipulation of the poor and needy in order to bankroll an opulent lifestyle. Lacking any empathy for others, they have an 'It's all about me' philosophy of life where others are but a means to an end. What's more, they demand their husbands

---

2. Denis Baly, *Geography of the Bible*, 2nd ed. (New York: Harper & Row, 1974), 220.
3. Rasmussen, 29.
4. William Sanford LaSor, 'Bashan,' in *The International Standard Bible Encyclopedia*, ed. Geoffrey W. Bromiley, rev. ed. [*ISBE*] (Grand Rapids: Eerdmans, 1979), 1:436-7; see also Deuteronomy 32:14; Jeremiah 50:19; Micah 7:14. Bashan was also noted for its oak trees (Isaiah 2:13; Ezekiel 27:6; Zechariah 11:2).
5. For instance, see Song of Solomon 4 and 7.
6. 'The Real Housewives of …' is a series of 'reality TV' shows depicting social circles of affluent women in cities or regions in the United States.

Amos 4:1-13

engage in whatever endeavors necessary to acquire more wealth. Amos depicts these divas as overbearing housewives commanding their husbands to bring them what they desire, no matter what the expense or means of getting it. While these women may not have been the ones actually physically taking the money and possessions from the poor, they were just as guilty as their husbands for the demands they were making on their husbands. The women's lust for self-gratification has no bounds. They are not unlike one of their former queens, Jezebel, who plotted against Naboth, having him killed so that she could seize his vineyard (1 Kings 21). Jezebel's life came to a gruesome end as a result of her wickedness (2 Kings 9:30-37).

Today, many Americans are consumed with 'The American Dream'—freedom to do or say what we want, to buy what we want, to be what we want. We are focused on our needs, desires, and perceived rights. We get on the fast-track wanting now what took our parents a lifetime to acquire through discipline and hard work, or we become so miserly and consumed with money it robs us of our very lives. God has been so good to us that we have started believing blessings and privileges are actually our rights. It reminds me of an illustration I heard a number of years ago. Suppose you were in your home and the doorbell rings. You open the door to find a plainly clothed gentleman holding a $100 bill in his hand. Without saying a word, he offers it to you. You take it, and he politely nods, turns, and walks away. The next day, at the very same time you hear your doorbell ring again. You open the door to find the very same gentleman holding another $100 bill in his hand. He gives it to you, nods, and walks away. This same turn of events happens each day, so much so that you begin anticipating his coming and are ready to open the door when the doorbell rings. On the thirty-first day the doorbell does not ring. You look out the window and see the man going to your neighbor's house across the street. You open the door and call out to the man about where is 'your' $100 bill. You have gotten so used to the money that you began to believe you were entitled to it, but in truth you never were entitled to it. It was given as a gift. God had been so good to Israel they began believing they were entitled to such wealth.

Also, note the demands they put upon their husbands. How many of us put undue pressure on our spouses to make more money so that they may help satisfy our materialistic cravings, so that we might live the American Dream? And how many of us are truly satisfied by what we get? It seems it is never enough. Often such demands on our spouses come with a detriment to his or her spiritual, relational, physical, and emotional well-being. In doing so, we sin against our spouses and against all others who are ill-affected by their actions to meet our demands. It is a self-centeredness that may be hidden from all others with the exception of our spouses, but we must remember it is not hidden from a holy God. There are consequences for such self-centeredness.

Amos announces the grim consequences to Samaria's divas for their self-absorption. The phrases—'behold, the days are coming upon you, when they shall take you away with hooks, even the last of you with fish-hooks'—in verse 2 have been interpreted in a number of ways because of the ambiguity of the Hebrew terms Amos uses. The first interpretation is that the women will be carried away in shields or boats.[7] Second, it could mean the women will be carried away in pots or baskets used to carry fish to market. This interpretation would mean that the women will be carried off into captivity or that their corpses will be carried away like fish that have been butchered.[8] Third, it could mean they will be dragged away by ropes.[9] Fourth, it may refer to hooks or fish-hooks hooked into the women to pull them along into captivity. The Assyrians sometimes put rings in the noses or lips of their captives and hooked chains into them as they led their captives in a line off into captivity.[10] Fifth, it could be using fish-hooks metaphorically, saying the women have been caught like fish on hooks. Sixth, in keeping with 'cows of Bashan,' the phrase could be referring to barbed prods used

---

7. G. R. Driver, 'Babylonian and Hebrew Notes,' *Die Welt des Orients* 2 (1954): 20-1.

8. Paul, 134; John H. Hayes, *Amos: The Eighth-Century Prophet: His Times and His Preaching* (Nashville: Abingdon, 1988), 140-1.

9. S. J. Schwantes, 'Notes on Amos 4:2b,' *Zeitschrift für die Alttestamentliche Wissenschaft* 79 (1967): 82-3.

10. Jan de Waard and William A. Smalley, *A Translator's Handbook on the Book of Amos* (New York: United Bible Societies, 1979), 79.

to drive cattle. Seventh, the hooks may be metaphorically referring to butchered cattle hanging on hooks. The Assyrian propensity for impaling their captives may support this notion.[11] Additionally, scholars are unsure as to the meaning of 'Harmon' in verse 3. It could mean Mt Hermon to the north, another unknown mountain, or even a dung pit, depending on how one understands the Hebrew text.[12] While there may be debate over the nature of these expressions Amos uses, it is certain that the people of his day understood the expressions, and there is no debate over their ultimate meaning. Like Jezebel before them, these divas of Samaria will suffer; some will perish, and others will be driven into exile. The walls that once stood in testimony to their wealth and glory will have such large breaches in them that the women will be driven straight out of the city through the gaping holes. The Lord has sworn this declaration by His own holiness. Therefore, it will happen. In 722 B.C., the Assyrians destroyed Samaria and carried its survivors into captivity.

Self-centeredness expresses itself by self-deception (4:4-5)
Amos now turns his attention to a second offence before the Lord. The worship of Israel had become superficial and self-exalting. Amos mockingly calls the people to their worship so that they can rebel against God. The people are busily involved in religious activities as they throng to their places of worship. Every morning they are offering their sacrifices. These sacrifices are supposed to be made for the atonement of sins and to symbolize fellowship with God, and the requirement is for them to be made only once or at most three times a year (see Leviticus 1–5).[13] The law states that the people are supposed to bring their tithes from the produce of their land every three years (Deut. 14:28-29), yet they are bringing tithes every three days. Amos encourages the people to bring their thanksgiving offerings of leavened bread. These sacrifices were supposed to be voluntary expressions of gratitude for God's blessing (Lev. 7:13-15). Furthermore, Amos directs the people to offer their freewill offerings. These

---

11. See Garrett's discussion concerning these seven possible interpretations, 111-13.
12. Paul, 135-6.
13. Honeycutt, 83.

were supposed to be voluntary offerings usually associated with a vow (Lev. 7:16). Why are the people so involved in these acts of worship? Why are they going beyond what the law requires? It is so they can boast about how pious they are before others. For them, acts of worship are about drawing attention and glory to themselves, not to God. If one could travel back to that time and watch Israel's worship one would be very impressed, yet God sees through their religious veneer. They may be successful in deceiving themselves about how pious they are and how pleased God must be with them, but the Lord is not deceived. Instead of pleasing God, their preoccupation with religious ceremonies serves to deepen the depth of their transgressions and intensify God's wrath. Their intentions are both hypocritical and boastful. They may impress others and themselves, but they fail to impress God. No amount of religious fervor can substitute for faithful obedience to God marked by a life of integrity. Furthermore, notice how they are not offering up sin offerings or guilt offerings. They lack any sense of guilt for their sin. They have deceived themselves into believing they are blameless before God. The absence of repentance in their worship should have given them pause, as it should to God's people today.

True worship is Christ-focused worship offered by His people who have clean hands and pure hearts (Ps. 24:3-4). Nevertheless, how many of us meet with others for a time of so-called worship where our priority is to be entertained and leave the place feeling better about ourselves? Or how much time do worship leaders spend trying to make sure they impress the congregation with their musical, intellectual, comical, homiletical, or even 'spiritual' abilities? Anything we do in worship to draw attention to ourselves and away from Christ is not worship at all. Even so, we applaud ourselves as we impress ourselves. I recently heard of a church that hired professional musicians to lead its worship, but these musicians were unbelievers. How can those who deny Christ worship Him? Apparently, the church did it so they could put on a good show. We are self-deceived if we believe the Lord will accept our worship as we approach Him with sin in our hearts (Ps. 66:18). As we go into a time of corporate worship our prayer should be that Christ receives all honor and glory.

If we truly exalt Christ in our worship, then when we walk away people may not be so impressed with us, but they will be impressed with our God.

Self-centeredness expresses itself by self-delusion (4:6-11)
Most likely, Israel's expectation of God's response to its vigorous religious activities and God's actual response to them were quite different. The people expected God to continue to bless them and make them prosperous; instead God levied upon them His curses, curses of which he had warned them in His covenant with Israel (see Deuteronomy 27-28). If Israel had been faithfully obedient to God and the covenant, the people would have experienced the blessings many of their forefathers had experienced. However, God's faithfulness to His covenant with Israel manifests itself not only in His dependability to bestow blessings upon His devoted and loyal people but also in His dependability to exact the covenant curses upon His irresponsible and disloyal people. God is ever trustworthy to keep His Word whether in blessing or judgment. In methodical fashion, Amos reveals seven ways God has responded to Israel's unfaithfulness. Through Amos, the Lord emphasizes His actions in contrast to Israel's activities. The purpose of the Lord's actions has been twofold: first, they served as God's discipline upon His people, and second, they served as calls to Israel to repent. Observe what the Lord did by way of deprivation, infliction, opposition, and utter destruction.[14]

(1) Deprivation (4:6-8)
First, God gave the people 'cleanness of teeth', a vivid way of describing a nationwide famine. The people should have recognized the famine was from God because of His warning of what would happen should they break the covenant (Deut. 28:47-48). This is not to say every famine is the result of God's punishment. When Abraham experienced a famine in the land of Canaan, there is no indication God sent it in order to punish Abraham (Gen. 12:10). However, God explicitly indicates in the covenant He will send famine as a

---

14. Motyer speaks of the three categories of deprivation, infliction, and opposition (97).

result of Israel's covenant unfaithfulness. For Israel, famine is a sign of its rebellion against God and His displeasure with His people. Nevertheless, the famine also was a sign of the Lord's tender mercies. His desire is for reconciliation with Israel, but Israel would not repent.

Second, the Lord deprived His people of water at the time they needed it the most. The harvest season of barley and then wheat came during the months of May and early June.[15] The lack of water three months prior to harvest meant their crops would fail. Once again, Israel should have known the drought was the result of its unfaithfulness to the Lord. The Lord painted a vivid picture of the drought that would come as a consequence of Israel's disloyalty (Deut. 28:23-24). To make matters worse, God sent rain on some fields and not on others. Not long ago the area in which I live experienced a storm where most businesses and residences in our community lost power for a number of days. A friend of mine told me how frustrated he was when all of the homes in his neighborhood had their electric restored with the exception of his house and the houses of his two neighbors. For some reason, it took the utility company several more days before they restored power to these three homes. My friend was frustrated because he could not understand why everyone else in this neighborhood got their power restored while the other three did not. It is difficult enough to be deprived of life's necessities, but the difficulty seems to be multiplied when those around us appear to be untouched by it. They might have asked, 'Why me, and why not him?' They failed to recognize God's hand was behind it. Those without water staggered from dehydration from one town to another in search of water, but their desperate quests were to no avail. Recently, I visited an area in Niger where the region has been experiencing a drought for four years. A gentleman came up to me and said, 'America is a great nation because it has so much water.' Before my visit to Niger, I might have listed a number of ways God has blessed America, but I doubt if water would have even made the list. My visit to Niger helped me realize how easy it is for me to take for granted God's blessings and how devastating a drought can

---

15. Simon J. Devries, 'Calendar,' in *Holman Illustrated Bible Dictionary*, eds. Chad Brand, Charles Draper, and Archie England, rev. ed. (Nashville: Holman Reference, 2003), 252.

be. The heat became intense and the ground became as hard as iron in Israel, yet all they had to do was turn away from their sin, turn to God, and He would have had mercy on His people (Deut. 28:23). No matter how difficult their circumstances, Israel's hearts were even harder than the ground below them.

(2) Infliction (4:9-10a)
Third, the Lord struck with disease crops that had survived the drought. The covenant warns Israel of this calamity (Deut. 28:22). Imagine having been one of those farmers whose crops did receive rain during the drought. Maybe they felt badly for those whose crops failed, but at least their crops would make it along with the promise of greater profit, given the losses of others. Imagine their sense of relief and hope and then their sense of despair as they helplessly watched their crops turn yellow, then brown, and wither away because of blight caused by a sirocco, a very warm wind that blew in from the Arabian Desert from the east and caused extensive crop failure. Others watched as the destructive work of worms caused mildew, which had about the same effect on the crops as the siroccos.[16]

Fourth, the Lord sent locusts upon Israel's vineyards and groves. Locusts consumed just about everything in their path, and the carcasses of the locusts often stopped up wells and obstructed streams, so causing massive devastation in an area, resulting in its desolation.[17] It is virtually impossible to stop a locust swarm once it has begun. Swarms of up to ten billion locusts periodically affect areas in Africa, southwest Asia, and southern Europe. Locusts have obliterated areas covering up to 400 square miles, leaving behind them a barren landscape.[18] Given Israel's society was highly dependent upon its agricultural production, a locust swarm would have been especially devastating as it was one of the greatest calamities to happen in the ancient Near East. The Lord warned them of the coming locusts, should Israel forsake its covenant with Him (Deut. 28:38). Nevertheless, the people refused to repent of their sin.

---

16. King, 111.
17. Philip J. King and Lawrence E. Stager, *Life in Biblical Israel* (Louisville: Westminster John Knox Press, 2001), 87.
18. G. L. Keown, 'Locust,' *The International Standard Bible Encyclopedia*, ed. Geoffrey W. Bromiley, rev. ed. (Grand Rapids: Eerdmans, 1986), 3:150.

Fifth, the Lord struck the people of Israel with a plague. The Hebrew word probably refers to bubonic plague.[19] The bubonic plague was one of antiquity's most dreaded diseases. It was passed on to humans by the rat-flea. Once an individual contracted the disease he became ill almost immediately. The symptoms included a high fever, shivering, pneumonia, and bleeding from mucous membranes. About twenty-four hours after one became infected, the lymph nodes under the armpits, in the groin, or on the neck swelled, forming buboes, which were similar in appearance to large blisters, and then the person died.[20] A biblical description of this plague is in 1 Samuel 5–6. As with the other incidents, the Lord had warned Israel of this plague as a result of its sin, but the people refused to learn their lesson.[21]

(3) Opposition (4:10b)
Sixth, the Lord used Israel's enemies in order to punish His people and call them back to himself. Amos describes the loss of Israel's elite soldiers, killed by the sword. Israel's enemies butchered these young men like the horses upon which they rode. What's more, this massacre happened so close to home that the people could smell the stench of the rotting corpses on the battlefield.[22] Their grief must have been unbearable, still Israel refused to return to the Lord. They disregarded God's warning in the *tôrâ* and failed to recognize their culpability for what had happened.[23]

(4) Destruction (4:11)
The seventh and climactic calamity involved fire. Some scholars believe verse 11 describes an earthquake that ignited a fire that was as destructive as the wiping out of Sodom and Gomorrah.[24] Others believe Amos is describing the results of Israel's military defeats, given the previous verse along

---
19. R. K. Harrison, 'דֶּבֶר,' in *New International Dictionary of Old Testament Theology & Exegesis*, ed. Willem A. VanGemeren (Grand Rapids: Zondervan Publishing House, 1997), 1:915.
20. Ibid.
21. Leviticus 26:25; Numbers 14:12; Deuteronomy 28:21; see also 2 Samuel 24:15; Ezekiel 14:19.
22. See Isaiah 34:3; Joel 2:20.
23. Leviticus 26:25; Deuteronomy 28:25.
24. Paul, 148-49.

with Amos' prolific use of the word 'fire' to denote a military defeat.[25] It probably refers to Israel's near extinction at the hands of the Syrians led by Hazael prior to Jeroboam's taking the throne of Israel.[26] The comparison to Sodom and Gomorrah may serve more than just the purpose of illustrating the extent of the destruction. It may indicate Israel's enemies sowed the ground with salt so that nothing could grow there anymore. The Assyrians appear to have practiced this act of retribution on their enemies quite often.[27] Therefore, it is reasonable to conclude others might have done the same to Israel. If so, like Sodom and Gomorrah, Israel became a wasteland of salt, sulphur, and ash. However, as deserving of these consequences as Israel was, the Lord graciously and mercifully saved a remnant of Israel before it was totally annihilated. Still, Israel refused to repent of its sin and turn to God.

Israel suffered all of these calamities, but the people were either too hard-hearted or so self-deluded by their false sense of righteousness they could not fathom God was displeased with them. Is it possible God sends calamities upon people and nations today to punish them for their sins and call them to Himself only for the people and nations to deem these tumultuous events random occurrences in nature? Sure, not every calamity happens as a direct consequence of particular sins. We live in a fallen world. On the other hand, we may be too quick to assume randomness when God is actually sending us a message, calling us to Himself. Many seem to believe only the God of the Old Testament would do such actions. These people fail to recognize the Lord is the same yesterday, today, and forever (Heb. 13:8).

Self-centeredness expresses itself by self-reliance (4:12-13)
Again, Amos surprises his audience. The seventh word of judgment normally would have been the climax and the last, but Amos has one more that surpasses all he has said up to this point. Because of Israel's self-centeredness and refusal to return to the Lord, there will be no more warnings and no more opportunities for reconciliation to God. They have

---
25. Niehaus, 402.
26. Garrett, 124.
27. Niehaus, 402.

relied on themselves and their own religious piety. They have demonstrated their self-confidence by living without the Lord. Now the Lord says they can continue to rely on themselves as they prepare to meet Him. Their unwillingness to come to God in repentance will result in His coming to them in judgment.

Who is this God with whom Israel must prepare to meet? First, He is Israel's God. He is the God who brought their forefather, Abraham, from a distant land and established him in Canaan. He is the God who brought Jacob and his family into Egypt as a small people and then brought Israel out of Egypt a great multitude. He is the God who redeemed them from slavery and called them into a covenant relationship with Himself. He is the God who made Israel His treasured possession. He is the God who made them a nation. He is the God who loves them. He is Israel's God.

Second, He is the Creator. He has created the mountains and the wind. How could Israel be so foolish as to disregard its covenant with the Lord who is the Creator and develop an attitude of self-reliance? He is the God who has the rightful authority and ability to execute judgment because He is the Creator.

Third, the Lord is the God who reveals Himself to people, especially to Israel. How could the people of Israel forsake the Lord who has graciously revealed Himself to them over and over again through His law, His prophets, and His mighty deeds done on Israel's behalf? Now He is revealing His intent to come in judgment.[28]

Fourth, the Lord is the one true Judge of the earth.[29] The shining light of Israel will be extinguished. The Lord's treading the mountains may depict ownership, it may depict subjugation, but surely it depicts God's judgment.[30]

This passage should be a reminder that one's opportunity to repent of sin and be reconciled to God will not last forever. There comes a point of no return. Therefore, it is necessary to respond to God's call when God issues it. Consider Jesus' story concerning opportunity and time:

---

28. The text could be translated 'he reveals man's thoughts'; however, Garrett's discussion cogently argues in this case it is God who is revealing His thoughts/intentions to man, 128; see Amos 3:7.
29. Genesis 18:25; John 5:22-27; 2 Corinthians 5:10.
30. B. Smith, 94; see Deuteronomy 11:24; Job 9:8; Deuteronomy 33:29; Psalm 91:13; Isaiah 63:3; Lamentations 1:15; Micah 1:3-4.

Amos 4:1-13

And he told this parable: 'A man had a fig tree planted in his vineyard, and he came seeking fruit on it and found none. And he said to the vinedresser, "Look, for three years now I have come seeking fruit on this fig tree, and I find none. Cut it down. Why should it use up the ground?" And he answered him, "Sir, let it alone this year also, until I dig round it and put on manure. Then if it should bear fruit next year, well and good; but if not, you can cut it down"' (Luke 13:6-9).

Israel's rebellion and unfruitfulness brought about judgment. One must never take for granted the grace God bestows through His invitation. We can be like Pharaoh in Moses' day, Israel in Amos' day, or the Pharisees in Jesus' day who hardened their hearts until it was no longer possible to come to God, or we can be like the tax collector who prayed, 'God, be merciful to me, a sinner' (Luke 18:13). Quoting Psalm 95:7-8 the writer of Hebrews says, 'Today, if you hear his voice, do not harden your hearts' (Heb. 4:7).

STUDY QUESTIONS

1. How real is the temptation to be self-indulgent among God's people today?

2. How much if any has an attitude of entitlement infiltrated the Church today?

3. How much do people pressure their spouses and other family members to make more money just to satiate materialistic cravings?

4. How does self-centeredness express itself in self-deception?

5. How does self-centeredness express itself in self-delusion?

6. How does self-centeredness express itself in self-reliance?

7. Who is the God Israel must prepare to meet?

6

Seek God, and Live
(Amos 5:1-17)

In an episode on the *Andy Griffith Show*, Sheriff Andy Taylor and Deputy Barney Fife were concerned for everyone's safety when they heard Otis Campbell, the town drunk, had purchased an automobile.[1] They were sure Otis would eventually drive while intoxicated. Deputy Fife kept an eye on Otis and one night found Otis passed out from drunkenness on his newly purchased vehicle. Andy and Barney devised a plan to scare Otis so that he would never consider drinking and driving. They brought Otis to the jailhouse and put him in the cell Otis normally went in when he was drunk. They splashed water on him to wake Otis and then pretended not to hear or see Otis. Andy and Barney discussed Otis' tragic accident how he was driving while drunk, swerved off the road into a creek and was killed. Then Andy got his guitar, and he and Barney sang a song of lament, mourning the loss of Otis. Otis even joined them as they sang. Overwhelmed by the news of his death, Otis then passed out again. When Andy and Barney woke him, Otis told them of the horrible 'nightmare' he had and how glad he was he had sold his car earlier that day because he was concerned that he might be tempted to drink and drive. Andy and Barney were pleased to hear this news.

---

1. This episode is episode 19 from the fourth season titled 'Hot Rod Otis.'

Like Otis Campbell, Israel hears of its own tragic death, but there is nothing humorous about this declaration. Like Andy and Barney, the prophet Amos also sings a song of mourning, but there is nothing fictional about its content. Given the end of the preceding chapter where Amos warns Israel it is going to experience God's judgment, it is appropriate to lament Israel's demise. How somewhat odd and irritating it must have been to Amos' audience to hear him speak of Israel's death when from their perspective there absolutely was nothing wrong and no impending danger. In fact, all seemed as well as they could hope.

Some scholars believe Amos presented this lament at one of Israel's celebratory religious feasts at one of its prominent sacred shrines.[2] If so, once again, Amos' message has a shock effect as he does the unexpected. As Israel meets to celebrate the blessed lives they are enjoying Amos sings a lament mourning Israel's death. Imagine hearing someone singing a song mourning the death of an individual only to discover that you are that individual. Imagine the nerve of a person pronouncing you dead when you are quite still alive. Amos' lament probably caused quite a stir.

In the Old Testament, laments are quite common. They are dirges mourning someone's loss. The Book of Lamentations mourns the destruction of Jerusalem and the loss of life that occurred with its fall. Laments are also frequent in the Psalms. The structure of this particular lament of Amos concerning Israel is in the form of a chiasm. Chiastic structures are prevalent in Semitic writings, especially in the Old Testament. A chiastic structure is where the first line of a text corresponds to the last line of the text, the second line corresponds to the next-to-last line, and so on, so that the passage reaches a climax in the middle or at its center. The emphasis of a passage having a chiastic structure is usually on the center element or elements. Taking into consideration its chiastic structure, one may outline Amos 5:1-17 the following way:

---

2. E. Hammershaimb, *The Book of Amos: A Commentary*, trans. J. Sturdy (Oxford: Basil Blackwell, 1970), 76; W. Rudolph, *Joel-Amos-Obadiah-Jonah* (Gütersloh: Gerd Mohn, 1971), 187; Paul, 159.

A Lament the death of the nation (vv. 1-3)
  B Call to seek God and live (vv. 4-6)
    C Accusations of no justice (v. 7)
      D Hymn to Yahweh (vv. 8-9)
    C' Accusations of no justice (vv. 10-13)
  B' Call to seek God and live (vv. 14-15)
A' Lament the death of the nation (vv. 16-17)[3]

So what is Amos' message as he puts forward this lament?

Those who reject the Lord are dead (5:1-3, 5, 7, 10-13, 16-17)
Jesus' description of the church of Sardis would be a fitting description of Israel during Amos' time: 'I know your works. You have the reputation of being alive, but you are dead' (Rev. 3:1). Outwardly, Israel did appear to be vibrant and alive. The large landowners and corporations of their day were prospering more than they ever had since the glory days of Solomon. They were growing superb vineyards with abundant productivity. As a result, many of the people were able to afford the construction of magnificent homes. Israel's fortifications were a reminder of recent victories on the battlefield and of a national security not known to Israel since the glory days of David and Solomon. Furthermore, there was probably no time in Israel's history when it was more active religiously than during this time. In so many ways, Israel must have relished in its prosperity and special position before God as His treasured possession.

However, Amos speaks of 'virgin Israel' as 'fallen and no more to rise' and as 'forsaken with no one to raise her up'. Not even the Lord would lift a finger to rescue her. The promise of a bright future for this budding nation is no more. Its army will be decimated to the point of near extinction.[4] The slaughter will be so great no family will go untouched. Wailing will rise up from every part of Israel, in all of the squares, in all of the streets, and in all of the vineyards. This triple repetition emphasizes the great extent of the wailing that will occur.[5] Those in the cities, the farmers in the fields,

---

3. G. Smith, *NIV Application Commentary*, 312; see also J. de Waard, 'The Chiastic Structure of Amos V:1-17,' *VT* 27 (1977): 170-7.
4. See Amos 2:14-16; 4:10; 7:11.
5. In the Old Testament, the threefold repetition of something is the Semitic way of expressing extreme emphasis, see Isaiah 6:3.

along with the professional mourners, will all mourn the loss of Israel's fathers, sons, brothers, and friends. Israel's army will cease to exist; therefore, Israel as a nation will cease to exist as well. While a remnant of people from the nation of Israel will survive, the survival of the northern kingdom of Israel as a self-governing nation will be no more.[6] As the Lord passed through Egypt at the time of the first Passover, so the Lord will 'pass through' Israel's 'midst' again (Exod. 12:12, 23), but this time it is Israel that will suffer the Lord's wrath. This time there will be no protection. All that will be left of the nation will be a deathly silence. But why? How has it come to this?

First, they substituted religion for authentic devotion to God. Apparently, the people were going to three sacred sites in order to perform religious acts. The first place Amos mentions is Bethel. Bethel was located near the southern border of the northern kingdom in Ephraim about twelve miles north of Jerusalem.[7] The place was especially significant to Jacob. It was at that location where he had his first encounter with the Lord, and the Lord reiterated to Jacob the promise He had made to Abraham and Isaac. The Lord said to Jacob, 'Behold, I am with you and will keep you wherever you go' (Gen. 28:15). Jacob called the place Bethel, meaning 'The House of God.' Later in his life, Jacob encountered the Lord at Bethel a second time. It was then the Lord said, 'Your name is Jacob; no longer shall your name be called Jacob, but Israel shall be your name.' So God called his name Israel and said to him, 'I am God Almighty: be fruitful and multiply. A nation and a company of nations shall come from you, and kings shall come from your own body. The land that I gave to Abraham and Isaac I will give to you, and I will give the land to your offspring after you' (Gen. 35:10-12). From that time forward Bethel became a sacred place for Jacob's descendants, and it represented a place of God's promised presence and blessing.

The second sacred place Amos mentions is Gilgal. Gilgal was located northeast of Jerusalem between Jericho and the

---

6. G. F. Hasel, *The Remnant: The History and Theology of the Remnant Idea from Genesis to Isaiah,* Andrews University Monograph Studies in Religion 5 (Berrien Springs, MI: Andrews University, 1972), 187-90.

7. W. Ewing and R. K. Harrison, 'Bethel,' in *The International Standard Bible Encyclopedia,* ed. Geoffrey W. Bromiley, rev. ed. (Grand Rapids: Eerdmans, 1979), 1:465-7.

Jordan River. Gilgal became a place of great significance to Israel.[8] It was the first place where the Israelites set up an encampment when they entered into the Promised Land under Joshua. It was there the Israelites erected a twelve-stone monument commemorating their miraculous crossing of the Jordan River on dry ground and their entrance into the Promised Land (Josh. 4:20). It was at Gilgal where the Israelites recommitted themselves as the people of God by circumcising the males and eating the first fruits of the Promised Land as the manna ceased (Josh. 5:2-12). Gilgal was the place where the Lord spoke personally to Joshua (Josh. 6:2) and promised him victory. It was from Gilgal Joshua launched his military campaign to conquer Canaan.[9] Gilgal was the place where Israel's first king, Saul, received confirmation of his kingship (1 Sam. 11:14-15). Gilgal represented Israel's rightful inheritance of the Promised Land, God's faithfulness to Israel to keep His promises, and Israel's victory over its enemies.

The third sacred shrine to which Amos refers is Beersheba. Beersheba was centrally located near the southern border of Judah in the Negev.[10] Beersheba received its name because of the covenant Abraham made with Abimelech, and it was at that time Abimelech told Abraham, 'God is with you in all that you do' (Gen. 21:22, 31-32). It was at Beersheba the Lord spoke to Isaac and said, 'I am the God of Abraham your father. Fear not, for I am with you and will bless you and multiply your offspring for my servant Abraham's sake' (Gen. 26:24). Furthermore, it was at Beersheba where the Lord spoke to Jacob promising, 'Jacob, Jacob.' And he said, 'Here am I.' Then he said, 'I am God, the God of your father. Do not be afraid to go down to Egypt, for there I will make you into a great nation. I myself will go down with you to Egypt, and I will also bring you up again, and Joseph's hand shall close your eyes' (Gen. 46:2-4). The past events at Beersheba associate God's presence with Israel's forefathers. Therefore, Beersheba represented God's promised presence to Israel.

---

8. W. H. Brownlee, 'Gilgal,' in *The International Standard Bible Encyclopedia*, ed. Geoffrey W. Bromiley, rev. ed. (Grand Rapids: Eerdmans, 1982), 2:470-2.
9. Joshua 5:13-15; 9:6; 10:6-43; 14:6.
10. A. F. Rainey, 'Beer-sheba,' in *The International Standard Bible Encyclopedia*, ed. Geoffrey W. Bromiley, rev. ed. (Grand Rapids: Eerdmans, 1979), 1:448-51.

It appears the people were trusting in the benefits these sacred places represented rather than in the Lord who made these promises. It is as if they believed that there was something mystical about these sacred shrines and if they traveled to them they could be assured that just as God was with the patriarchs God would be with them. It seems their pilgrimages to these places were all about God's blessing them. How many people do similar things today? Throngs of people travel to the Holy Land seeking some kind of mystical experience or special blessing from God. Others believe if they could just attend a certain conference or sit under the teaching or ministry of some renowned pastor or teacher they could receive some special anointing of God.

For Israel, it was all about them. It never dawned on them that as they received the Lord's blessings their lives and worship should be pleasing to God. Of course, we do need God's blessing, but the Lord Himself says we are to seek first His kingdom and righteousness and all these other things will be added to us (Matt. 6:33). Their question was 'What is in it for me?' It is that same kind of consumerism that has crept its way into the Church today. Many of us attend church asking, 'What is in it for me?' It is all about our being blessed. I wonder how many faithful missionaries around the world, who serve in very difficult circumstances, asked that question as they entered the field? If they did so from the perspective of the world, then many have made grave errors of judgment because they later suffered from opposition and various maladies. How many of us attend local houses of worship with the intention of being a blessing to God and to others? It involves seeking to please God without any strings attached, giving without obligating or strong-arming God to give us what we want or think we need. It involves serving God by serving others.

Not only did Israel substitute religion for devotion to God, but secondly, the people substituted rhetoric for reality. The people of Israel declared the Lord was with them (5:14), yet the Lord indicated He is not with Israel. Their sacred places were their security blankets because of what these places represented to Israel. They seemed to believe that if they continued saying God was with them then He was. Recently,

Amos 5:1-17

I saw a segment on the news where a mental health expert was saying that positive thinking has become a detriment to many people in our society. Many are persuaded that if they just believe strongly enough and declare something to be true long enough, then it will happen. The mental health expert said this is not necessarily true. The repetition of some mantra will not change reality. The following story illustrates this truth. There were three ministers in a boat. The first was a Calvinist, the second was an Arminian, and the third was one who always spoke of the power of positive thinking. The boat capsized, and all three of the men drowned. When they came to, they realized they were not in heaven. The Calvinist said, 'I thought I had eternal life, but apparently I did not.' The Arminian said, 'I thought I had eternal life, but it appears I lost it.' The positive thinking minister closed his eyes and said, 'I am not here, and it is not hot.' We might repeat whatever pious or positive sayings we want to repeat to make us feel better, but repeating a saying will not make what we desire a reality. The greatest desire of the people of Israel was that God was with them. Today, one might say, 'God is with me.' As important a declaration as that is, just as important is the declaration made by our hearts, our lips, and our actions that 'We are with God.' The people of Amos' day wanted to look like they loved the Lord, to talk like they loved the Lord, and to even worship like they loved the Lord, but they did not truly love the Lord. They cared only for themselves.

Third, they practiced injustice and profited from others who were unjust. The wealthy took advantage of the needy, and the needy had no recourse. There was no one with the authority and power to defend them. The sweetness of justice had been turned into wormwood, a plant with a bitter taste. By Israel's rejection of the Lord, they hurled to the ground the righteousness once elevated before them, a righteousness demonstrated by God's character in the midst of His people and expressed by His instruction to them. Those who courageously upheld justice and truth became the objects of hate, ridicule, and oppression. The privileged illegally taxed the underprivileged in order to support their opulent lifestyles. They manipulated the courts with bribes.

It is as if the mafia were running Israel's entire society. Every decision the wealthy made was based upon self-interest. They only helped those who one day could return the favor. However, if a person had nothing to offer them, then the nobles of Israel withheld from him any favor. Their concern for themselves surpassed their desire to do what was morally right. They appeared to live by the motto by which many live today, 'If it is in my self-interest, then it is right.' However, Amos' message was 'If it is right, then it is in your self-interest.'

Those who seek the Lord will live (5:4-6, 14-15)
Israel has received the pronouncement of its death, and has heard Amos' lament. Nevertheless, the one who 'gives life to the dead' (Rom. 4:17) exhorts the dead people of Israel to seek Him and live. First, the Lord tells Israel to seek Him and not empty religion. Do not seek sacred places; seek Me. Do not repeat mantras such as 'God is with us' or 'We are God's treasured possession' and substitute them for true love, devotion, and obedience to the Lord. In the denomination in which I grew up and to which I still belong I have heard many people say something like, 'I walked the aisle, I prayed the prayer and was baptized. Therefore, I am going to heaven.' Yet their lives reveal no evidence of love and devotion to the Lord Jesus Christ. Many are counting on religious rites and activities devoid of true change in one's heart and actions for a right standing with God. They fail to realize 'if anyone is in Christ, he is a new creation. The old has passed away; behold, the new has come' (2 Cor. 5:17). Others who are quite active in the church are like those of whom the Lord Jesus Christ speaks when He says,

> Beware of false prophets, who come to you in sheep's clothing but inwardly are ravenous wolves. You will recognize them by their fruits. Are grapes gathered from thornbushes, or figs from thistles? So, every healthy tree bears good fruit, but the diseased tree bears bad fruit. A healthy tree cannot bear bad fruit, nor can a diseased tree bear good fruit. Every tree that does not bear good fruit is cut down and thrown into the fire. Thus you will recognize them by their fruits. Not everyone who says to me, 'Lord, Lord,' will enter the kingdom of heaven, but the one who

does the will of my Father who is in heaven. On that day many will say to me, 'Lord, Lord, did we not prophesy in your name, and cast out demons in your name, and do many mighty works in your name?' And then will I declare to them, 'I never knew you; depart from me, you workers of lawlessness' (Matt. 7:15-23).

Like Israel, those who substitute religious activities for true devotion to God are in store for a great disappointment. All such substitutes lead to captivity and death.

Second, the Lord says, 'Seek good and not evil; love good and hate evil.' Seeking good and hating evil is a characteristic of one who loves the Lord. John says, 'Beloved, do not imitate evil but imitate good. Whoever does good is from God; whoever does evil has not seen God' (3 John v. 11). The fact that these nobles of Israel were continually rejecting the Lord and oppressing their neighbors was evidence they were not truly children of God, regardless of their profession. The Lord's exhortation displays His kindness to a rebellious people deserving of judgment.

When the Lord exhorts Israel to seek good and to love good, what is 'good'? Amos tells them it means to 'establish justice in the gate' (5:15). In other words, it means to uphold God's standard of moral and ethical behavior in relationship to others.[11] The prophet Micah elaborates on what is good, saying, 'He has told you, O man, what is good; and what does the LORD require of you but to do justice, and to love kindness, and to walk humbly with your God?' (Micah 6:8). 'To do justice' means to walk with God so much that His standards of right and wrong become His followers' standards of right and wrong. 'To love kindness' means that God's followers, as people who have received His kindness and mercy, are to exhibit such kindness and mercy to others. Note how God's people are to act justly themselves but are to show kindness and mercy when it comes to others. 'To walk humbly with your God' means His followers are to live lives marked by an unwavering loyalty to Him and focused upon loving and pleasing Him.[12]

Those in the Church should ask upon what is their focus. Imagine a 2x4 piece of lumber on the ground and someone

---

11. Paul, 177.
12. Thomas J. Finley, *Everyman's Bible Commentary: Joel, Obadiah, and Micah* (Chicago: Moody Press, 1996), 169-70.

asked you to walk from one end of it to the other. If you were in reasonably good health, it would probably pose no difficulty. However, imagine that same 2x4 placed ten stories up in the air and someone again asked you to walk from one end of the board to the other. You might be looking for something to help you get across it, but the only way across will be to have all of your focus on the board. Looking away from the board will only lead to disaster. God's call to Israel was to seek Him and live. All other ways of life would lead to Israel's disaster, and they did.

Amos' exhortation to hate evil is to hate all that is in opposition to that which is good. Too often those of us who are evangelicals emphasize seeking good, but we often neglect the imperative to hate evil. It is almost as if we are to love good, but it is fine to be ambivalent toward evil. We see the fallenness of our world all around us and become so used to it that it fails to evoke any sense of disgust. Instead of justice being turned into bitter wormwood, it is injustice and wickedness that should give God's people a bitter distaste and revulsion. Why? The reason is because these things are repulsive to God.

Those who ignore the Lord do so at their own peril (5:8-9)

The chiastic structure of the text reveals the emphasis of this message is not on Israel but on the Lord, the one responsible for Israel's death. This central section of Amos' message is a hymn declaring the magnificent sovereignty and power of God. First, He is the one who controls the seasons. The constellations Pleiades and Orion were associated with the New Year and the change of the winter and summer seasons which, of course, affected the agricultural cycle.[13] The earth and its seasons, upon which Israel is dependent, are dependent upon the Lord God. Furthermore, it is the Lord who is in control of the earth's days and nights. Every day all of creation is dependent upon God's consistent rule. Also, the Lord is in control of the waters on the earth either for the provision of life through the rains or the destruction of life through floods. It is this God whom Israel must prepare to meet. It is this God

---

13. G. Fohrer, *Das Buch Hiob*, KAT 16 (Gütersloh: Gerd Mohn, 1963), 216; Paul, 168.

who is coming to judge His people. It is this God who has exhorted His people to seek Him and live. It is this God who is in control of the future.

Israel thought it could be in control. Its recent military victories and its impressive defensive fortifications convinced Israel it was invincible against its enemies. No one but Amos would question its military national security. In Amos' day, in order to defend against the Assyrians' massive battering rams, the walls of the cities took the form of offset-inset walls, where one section stuck out and then the next section of wall would be set back. These angles in the walls allowed the defenders more control over their positions in combat. Archeologists have discovered cities in Israel, such as Dan, Hazor, and Megiddo, which had this kind of fortification.[14] They did everything possible to defend themselves against their enemies.

During times of peace these fortifications were used to store the people's goods. Many of their city walls were casemate walls. Casemate walls appear to date back to about the time of Solomon. Casemate walls were actually two walls going around the city with a space of about five to six feet between the two walls.[15] If an enemy approached the city, the people filled in the space with earth and rocks. When the enemy breached the wall they were met with the earth and gravel coming down through the hole. In order to continue through the breach, the enemy would have to deal with the rubble and attempt to break through a second wall while at the same time deal with the defenders attacking them. These casemate walls were divided by partitions with small chambers used for storage during peacetime. Therefore, as the nobles of Israel gazed at their magnificent fortifications, the walls not only reminded them their lives were secure but also their material possessions appeared to be secure. Israel's fortifications gave the people a sense of security in another way too. To have such a formidable army and such massive fortifications must have led the people to believe God truly was with them. Surely, they had convinced themselves that these defences were testaments to God's good pleasure with Israel.

---

14. King, 72.
15. Ibid.

Nevertheless, the Lord indicates He will bring down the strong and destroy Israel's fortresses. The people are not in control of their lives; they are not in control of their possessions; and they are not in control of their eternities. Instead of being independent, Israel has been altogether dependent upon the Lord, even though Israel has failed to recognize this truth. The Lord who is the creator and sovereign over His creation is in control of all that concerns Israel. It is the Lord who made Israel, and it is the Lord who will bring her down.

In 1897, a journalist received news that Mark Twain was deathly ill. When he went to see Twain he discovered it was Twain's cousin who was sick and not Twain. Contrary to popular belief, no one published Twain's obituary at that time. However, Twain recounted the incident in an issue of the *New York Journal* on June 2, 1897. It is in this account Twain penned his famous words, 'The report of my death is an exaggeration' (which is usually misquoted as 'The rumors of my death have been greatly exaggerated' or 'The reports of my death are greatly exaggerated'). In Israel's case, the report of its death is no exaggeration. Nonetheless, the Lord's declaration of Israel's demise contains a call of reconciliation to Israel. Speaking of the Lord, the writer of Chronicles says, 'If you seek him, he will be found by you, but if you forsake him, he will forsake you' (2 Chron. 15:2). If only the people in Amos' day had responded to the Lord's invitation to seek Him and live! If only people today would respond to the Lord's invitation to seek Him and live!

STUDY QUESTIONS

1. Is it possible there are times when God's people are celebrating when they should be mourning? If so, when?

2. How do people substitute religion for authentic devotion to God?

3. How can looking to past manifestations of God's work become a substitute for fervent devotion to God in the present?

4. How can obsession over symbols of God's blessing become a replacement for true commitment to God?

5. How did a spirit of consumerism infiltrate Israel? Does it do so in the Church today?

6. How can religious rhetoric become a stumbling block to God's people?

7. How did Israel's self-effort become a substitute for trust in the Lord?

7

Confidence Isn't Everything
(Amos 5:18-27)

Josiah Leming was a contestant in the 2008 season of *American Idol*, a popular singing contest broadcast on the Fox television network. Josiah was an eighteen-year-old who lived in his car and sang with a fake British accent. He performed three times. The first two performances were well received, but the third performance fell short of expectations, with the judges telling him that he had become overconfident. Josiah denied being overconfident, but in an interview just before he went before the judges to see if he had made the final cut to go to Hollywood, he indicated that he believed himself to be a shoo-in to move on in the contest and he expected to have a great time in *American Idol*. However, when Josiah went before the judges his expectations were crushed as they told him he was eliminated from the contest.

The people in Amos' day were a lot like Josiah Leming. They too were confident in their success, but Amos indicated that they were self-deceived. Their self-deception revolved around three misconceptions: (1) the Day of the Lord would be a day of salvation for them (5:18-20); (2) they could be secure in their relationship with God because of their worship and offerings to Him (5:21-27); and (3) they could trust in their affluence and strong military to provide them security from their enemies (6:1-14). In Amos 5:18-27, Amos confronts the first two of these three misconceptions and raises three questions to his listeners: (1) Does your future truly hold what you believe it holds? (2) Is your worship of the Lord truly worship of the Lord? and (3) Is the Lord truly your God?

Does your future hold what you believe it holds? (5:18-20) The people of Israel in Amos' day apparently believed their future was bright. This belief was demonstrated by their desire for the coming Day of the Lord, which must have been a well-established concept by the time of Amos, even though he is the first of the prophets to use this expression (v. 18). They seemed to believe the Day of the Lord would be a time of deliverance for the nation of Israel and a time of reckoning and destruction for her enemies. The concept of the Day of the Lord may have been linked to past military victories Israel experienced because of the Lord's miraculous intervention, such as Gideon's victory over the Midianites or David's defeat of the Philistines. The people continued to celebrate such victories in their worship (e.g. Psalm 136), increasing Israel's expectations of future victories.[1] Indeed, in one sense they were correct about the Day of the Lord. The Day of the Lord would be a time of national deliverance. It would be a time of reckoning and judgment for the enemies of God and the enemies of His people in fulfillment of His covenant with Abraham.

So why did Amos raise the question concerning their longing for the Day of the Lord? Given the many difficulties Israel had endured at the hands of her enemies, why should she not long for such a day? Amos himself was quite aware of the atrocities Israel suffered at the hands of the surrounding nations (1:3–2:3). Why should the people not long for the day when they will see God's eternal kingdom established in their midst and they experience the eternal blessings of God? What was the problem? The problem was that the vast majority of people in Amos' day were self-deceived in believing that they were right with God and therefore safe from God's coming wrath when in fact they had become enemies of God themselves (cf. 9:10). Their perception of their standing before God became so warped, they believed only blessing could come to them from the Lord, and the Day of the Lord would be that climactic

---

1. David Allan Hubbard, *Joel and Amos: An Introduction and Commentary* (Leicester, England: Inter-Varsity Press,1989), 178-9.

event where God would declare before the nations, 'This is my beloved son in whom I am well-pleased.' One might imagine their singing the following words as they anticipated the Day of the Lord: 'When we all get to heaven, What a day of rejoicing that will be!' or 'In the sweet by and by, We shall meet on that beautiful shore' or 'When the trumpet of the Lord shall sound and time shall be no more, and the morning breaks eternal bright and fair; When the saved on earth shall gather over on the other shore, and the roll is called up yonder I'll be there.' The form of the Hebrew word translated 'desire' in verse 18 often means 'desire selfishly, lust, crave.'[2] Here it refers to a selfishly motivated desire to see the Day of the Lord. As descendants of Abraham, Israel was convinced the Day of the Lord would be a time of blessing and rejoicing as God would finally vindicate her and deliver her from her enemies.

Yet they would be sadly disappointed because the people had become like the foreign nations. Surely, the Day of the Lord would be a day of deliverance, but this deliverance would be for a faithful remnant. Just because they were descendants of Abraham and God's chosen people did not mean they were exempt from God's judgment. Therefore, Israel's anticipation for the Day of the Lord perplexed Amos. John the Baptist dealt with the same kind of attitude in his own day when he said, 'And do not presume to say to yourselves, "We have Abraham as our father," for I tell you, God is able from these stones to raise up children for Abraham. Even now the axe is laid to the root of the trees. Every tree therefore that does not bear good fruit is cut down and thrown into the fire' (Matt. 3:9-10). How many people believe their future is secure based upon the faith of their parents? Scripture makes it clear that the one who depends on the faith of one's parents for salvation will be greatly disappointed. Each of us is accountable to God for our faith in Him and faithfulness to Him.

Amos reinforces this message of future calamity with an illustration that would be humorous were it not so serious (v. 19). He says the Day of the Lord will be like a man who

---

2. William C. Williams, 'אוה,' in the *New International Dictionary of Old Testament Theology & Exegesis*, ed. Willem A. VanGemeren (Grand Rapids: Zondervan, 1997), 1:305; see Num 11:4, 34; Prov. 13:4; 21:26; 23:3, 6; 24:1; Deut. 5:21.

spots a lion and is relieved to escape from this danger only to run into a bear. The man somehow escapes the bear and finally makes it home. As he leans his hand against the wall in relief once again, a serpent that had somehow made its way into the house strikes him. Talk about having a bad day, but that is precisely Amos' point. The Day of the Lord will be a day of unavoidable disaster and inevitable judgment. As Shalom Paul says, 'Momentary success is only illusionary.'[3] There would be no escape for Israel.

Amos concluded his warning about the Day of the Lord with another question that reiterates what he has already said in verse eighteen (v. 20). Because of their disobedience to God a very dark day awaits them (cf. Deut. 28:28-29). This is another way of saying that for them that day will be a day of destruction and not deliverance. The people in Amos' day had understood what would happen on the Day of the Lord. Nevertheless, they had deceived themselves into believing that they were the ones who would be saved on that day when in fact they would be the objects of God's wrath. Contrary to their expectations, for them the Day of the Lord would be a day of danger and darkness, not safety and light. Their anticipation will turn into anxiety, and their great hope will transform into great harm.

Are people today so different from the people of Amos' day? Who among us believes our future holds judgment before almighty God? In 2003, George Barna reported, 'Most Americans do not expect to experience Hell first-hand: just one-half of 1% expect to go to Hell upon their death. Nearly two-thirds of Americans (64%) believe they will go to Heaven.'[4] If this idea holds true among Americans in general, how much more is it true of those in the church? We anticipate the second coming of Christ, but for how many of us will it be a day of darkness and not light? How many of us attest to a faith in Christ that is really non-existent, who have an appearance of godliness but deny the power thereof (2 Tim. 3:5)? It would do all of us well to examine ourselves to see if we have placed our faith in externalities or placed it in Jesus Christ alone for our salvation. Do we love the *idea* of following the Lord Jesus

---

3. Paul, 186.
4. George Barna, 'Americans Describe Their Views About Life After Death' [online], accessed 25 February 2008, http://www.barna.org; Internet.

Christ, or do we truly love Him. Will we hear the words, 'Well done, faithful servant,' or 'Depart from me, I never knew you'? Does our future hold what we believe it holds?

Is your worship of the Lord truly worship of the Lord? (5:21-25)

Amos 5:21-24 demonstrates that the Lord's declaration of judgment upon Israel was not because of her lack of religious fervor. The people were actively observing religious feasts and assemblies. The feasts were the three pilgrimages required by the law: the Feast of Unleavened Bread, the Feast of Harvest (also called the Feast of Weeks in Exodus 34:22 and Pentecost in the New Testament), and the Feast of Ingathering.[5] These feasts were 'to be focused on Yahweh, not on the people themselves, and therefore by implication would be covenant worship festivals rather than mere celebrations or national history or harvest festivals.'[6] The Feast of Unleavened Bread commemorated the Passover and Israel's hasty Exodus from Egypt.[7] It was a celebration of God's deliverance of Israel as He brought them into a covenant relationship with Himself at Mt. Sinai. The Feast of Harvest became known as the Feast of Weeks and Pentecost because the people were to celebrate it seven weeks after Passover, or 'fifty days to the day after the seventh Sabbath' (Lev. 23:16). This feast commemorated God's gracious deliverance of Israel from her enemies and covenant faithfulness. Also, it recognized God's gracious provision for His people with another wheat harvest.[8] The third feast is called the Feast of Ingathering, the Feast of Booths, or the Feast of Tabernacles.[9] It commemorated the Lord's protection and provision when Israel wandered in the wilderness for forty years before entering the Promised Land. It symbolized Israel's renewed commitment to the Lord and dependency upon His continued guidance and protection.[10] The assemblies

---

5. See Exodus 23:14-17; 34:22-23, 25.
6. Douglas K. Stuart, *Exodus*, The New American Commentary, vol. 2 (Nashville: Broadman and Holman Publishers, 2006), 534.
7. See Exodus 12:1-28; 13:6-10.
8. Stuart, 535-6; see Lev. 23:16-21; Num 28:26.
9. See Lev. 23:33-43; Deut. 16:13-15.
10. Neil S. Wilson and Linda K. Taylor, *Tyndale Handbook of Bible Charts and Maps* (Wheaton: Tyndale House Publishers, 2001), 30.

were gatherings for the purpose of prayer and sacrifice during holidays or times of trouble.[11] Each feast commemorated God's gracious covenant He had made with Israel and symbolized Israel's commitment to the Lord and His covenant. However, what these feasts symbolized and the reality in Israel were quite different because Israel was unfaithful to the covenant. Consequently, the Lord says, 'I hate, I despise your feasts, and I take no delight in your solemn assemblies' (v. 21).

Not only were the people of Israel faithful to observe the three major feasts, also they were actively offering sacrifices according to God's instruction. The first sacrifice Amos mentions is the burnt offering. It is the most common sacrifice in the Old Testament and mentioned more times than any of the other sacrifices. What makes this sacrifice unique is that the fire of the altar is supposed to completely consume the animal and not just certain parts of the animal as with the other sacrifices. The term 'whole burnt offering' elsewhere emphasizes the sacrifice is completely consumed by fire.[12] The burning of the whole animal means it all belongs to the Lord, so representing the total devotion to the Lord of the one offering the sacrifice.[13] The second sacrifice, the grain offering, is a gift made to ensure good relations with the Lord or to appease Him when he has been wronged.[14]

The third sacrifice Amos mentions is the peace offering. With a peace offering, the fat surrounding the kidneys, liver, and entrails along with the two kidneys and the lobe of the liver of the animal is totally consumed by fire, symbolizing the Lord's consumption of it; it was food for the Lord.[15] Next, the one making the sacrifice gives part of the animal to the priest to eat, and the family and friends of the worshipper join him in eating the rest of it. It is the only sacrifice where the people themselves participate in eating it. The fat belonging to the Lord and the remainder being consumed by the priest

---

11. See Leviticus 23:36; Numbers 29:35; Deuteronomy 16:8; 2 Kings 10:20; Isaiah 1:13; Joel 1:14; 2:15; Nehemiah 8:18.
12. See Deuteronomy 33:10; 1 Samuel 7:9; Psalm 51:19.
13. Robert I. Vasholz, *Leviticus: A Mentor Commentary* (Ross-Shire, Great Britain: Christian Focus Publications, 2007), 32.
14. Jacob Milgrom, *Leviticus 1–16*, The Anchor Bible, vol. 3 (New York: Doubleday, 1991), 196-7.
15. Leviticus 3:11, 16.

and the worshippers symbolizes the bond between them all within the covenant. By sharing in this sacrifice with God, the worshipper demonstrates his union with the Lord.[16]

However, like the feasts and assemblies, the Lord rejected Israel's sacrifices. Contrary to what the burnt offering symbolized, the people were far from being totally devoted to the Lord. Most likely, the people offered their grain offerings in order to ensure what they believed to be ongoing good relations with the Lord. Even if they did say their grain offerings were to appease God, there was no true repentance that accompanied their sacrifices. Furthermore, their persistent unfaithfulness to their covenant with the Lord demonstrated the people had no union with the Lord nor did they truly desire one. They had no peace with God, and they had no fellowship with their impoverished neighbors. Their sacrifices were all a sham, meaningless; therefore, they were all unacceptable to the Lord.

Furthermore, their meetings of worship incorporated melodious music with words no doubt praising the Lord. Music was an important part of Israelite worship, filled with singing and the playing of a number of instruments (Ps. 150). Stringed instruments especially played a significant part of Israelite worship. The two stringed instruments in the Old Testament are the *kinnor* (most often translated 'lyre') and the *nebel* (most often translated 'harp'). Technically, both were lyres. The lyre has a rectangular soundbox, two asymmetrical arms, and a slanting crossbar. What distinguishes a lyre from a harp is the harp lacks the crossbar.[17] These instruments were usually made of wood, yet some historians would say these lyres were also made of silver or ivory as well. The musicians played the *kinnor* during both non-religious and religious occasions. The *kinnor* was the smaller of the two lyres, having four to eight strings, and David and the Levites played it.[18] The larger, thicker lyre was the *nebel*, and it is this lyre to which Amos refers in verse 23. The *nebel* had ten to twelve strings, and the people usually reserved it for Israel's gatherings of worship.[19]

---

16. Vasholz, 45-6.
17. King and Stager, 291; the British Museum has a reconstructed Sumerian royal lyre from Ur dating to the third millennium.
18. King, 154.
19. King and Stager, 291-2.

Where the Lord once invited His people to praise Him with their music and delighted in their praise, He now says it is a noisy racket and that He will no longer listen to it. Why? It is because their expressions of worship through song had become as much a charade as the rest of Israel's expressions of worship had become.

When I was in seminary, I was the pastor of a very traditional church with a number of people who had professed to follow Christ for many years. In one particular message I emphasized the importance of what we say and do in worship matching up with what we actually believe and practice in our lives. As an example, I said the words we sing should be an expression of what we truly believe and live. We lack integrity if we do otherwise. A gentleman approached me after the service and said, 'Pastor, I do not know what the big deal is. They are just songs.' His attitude expresses what was part of Israel's problem and what is the problem for many others in the Church today. There is a disconnect between what is outwardly expressed in worship and its significance. What we do in worship should be an expression of what is in our hearts and practiced in our daily lives. Inconsistency of lifestyle or indifference in the heart is an affront to God when it comes to worshiping Him.

Amos' message was that before the Lord would delight in Israel's expressions of corporate worship, Israel needed to be a people who practiced justice and delighted in righteousness. The greatest and most valued resource in the ancient Near East was water. One could live without a number of things, but obviously one could not survive without water. Many times, water was in low supply. The Lord's message to Israel was clear: just as they could not expect to survive without the flow of precious water in her land, so the nation would not survive apart from faithful and moral obedience to the Lord. They were inundating Him with rivers of religiosity when He wanted from them rivers of justice and righteousness (v. 24). Not only did God desire professions of faith in Him when His people came together to worship Him, but He desired expressions of faith in Him in their daily lives as they cared for one another.

Not long ago two sports commentators were having a debate concerning a former coach who is renowned for his winning record, his tirades in practices and games, and his prolific use of profanity. The coach recently took a position as a sports analyst with a major television network. The two commentators were debating whether or not the coach would slip and use profanity on the air. The argument of one of the commentators caught my attention. He said he believed the coach would not slip because, like the coach, the two commentators themselves commonly used profanity in their conversations when off the air and had never slipped, so why should the coach? I had watched these two commentators for years, and because they had never used any profanity on their program, I was surprised by their revelation concerning their speech off the air. They never seemed to be the kind of men to use such language. It dawned on me, what I saw each week was their television persona, but it was not really who they were. When the people of Israel gathered together, they put on their worship personas. The missing ingredient in their worship was authenticity manifested in a lifestyle of faithful obedience. They were going through all the motions, but their worship lacked authenticity. They might have fooled others who watched them, but the Lord was not fooled. C. H. Spurgeon keenly observed:

> Men will attend to the most multiplied and minute ceremonial regulations—for such things are *pleasing to the flesh*—but true religion is too humbling, too heart-searching, too thorough for the tastes of the carnal men; they prefer something more ostentatious, flimsy, and worldly. Outward observances are *temporarily comfortable;* eye and ear are pleased; self-conceit is fed, and self-righteousness is puffed up: but they are *ultimately delusive,* for in the article of death, and at the day of judgment, the soul needs something more substantial than ceremonies and rituals to lean upon. Apart from vital godliness all religion is utterly vain; offered without a sincere heart, every form of worship is a solemn sham and an impudent mockery of the majesty of heaven.[20]

The only thing people can see is the outward appearance, but the Lord sees into the heart (1 Sam. 16:7).

In order to emphasize the truth that religious activities are not at the heart of the Lord's requirement for His people, He

---

20. C. H. Spurgeon, *Spurgeon's Daily Meditations*, accessed December 18, 2009; available from http://www.spurgeon.org/daily.htm; Internet.

brings their attention to their forty-year wanderings in the wilderness (v. 25). During that time the Lord God guided, protected, and provided for the children of Israel. All of His blessings upon His people were in no way linked to or the result of any religious activities on their part. The Lord's question, 'Did you bring to me sacrifices and offerings during the forty years in the wilderness, O house of Israel?' expected an answer of 'No.' Yet the absence of sacrifices and offerings in the wilderness had no negative impact on the people's relationship to the Lord. The Lord God continued to lead them (2:10). Therefore, Israel's relationship with the Lord was not contingent upon her obedience to any elaborate system of sacrifices and offerings, but exclusively and uniquely upon a devotion to the Lord expressed by absolute love for God and a love for one's neighbor as oneself.[21]

David understood this truth when he said, 'For you will not delight in sacrifice, or I would give it; you will not be pleased with a burnt offering. The sacrifices of God are a broken spirit; a broken and contrite heart, O God, you will not despise' (Ps. 51:16-17). Some might argue both Amos and David indicate the Lord did not want Israel to offer sacrifices. Such a notion could not be farther from the truth. For instance, David later says in Psalm 51, the Lord 'will delight in right sacrifices, in burnt offerings and whole burnt offerings; then bulls will be offered on your altar' (Ps. 51:19). The Lord will delight in sacrifices and offerings when the people who offer them are completely devoted to the Lord. The problem was not Israel's making sacrifices. The problem was they substituted their sacrifices in the place of sacrificial living before a holy God.

Is the Lord truly your God? (5:26-27)
Moreover, the people in Amos' day thought they could worship the Lord and worship other gods at the same time, but they were mistaken. A god is that which a person loves, trusts, and serves above all else. Therefore, logically, an individual can only have one true god. The first god the Lord mentions, Sikkuth, has been identified with the Babylonian name for Saturn or as an Assyrian god of war.[22] Kiyyun was an Assyrian

---

21. Paul, 193.
22. Finley, 225; Niehaus, 433.

god named for Saturn. Notice how the Lord says these are 'your images that you have made for yourselves'. Idols give authority to those who make them. The god becomes what one wishes it to be so that the idolater becomes like the god he serves.[23] Christopher Wright comments:

> At the root, then, of all idolatry is human rejection of the Godness of God and the finality of God's moral authority. The fruit of that basic rebellion is to be seen in many other ways in which idolatry blurs the distinction between God and creation, to the detriment of both.
> Idolatry dethrones God and enthrones creation. Idolatry is the attempt to limit, reduce and control God by refusing his authority, constraining or manipulating his power to act, having him available to serve our interests.... A great reversal happens: God, who should be worshiped, becomes an object to be used; creation, which is for our use and blessing, becomes the object of our worship.[24]

Consider too these words of Martin Luther:

> A god means that from which we are to expect all good and to which we are to take refuge in all distress, so that to have a God is nothing else than to trust and believe Him from the [whole] heart; as I have often said that the confidence and faith of the heart alone make both God and an idol.
> Thus, for example, the heathen who put their trust in power and dominion elevated Jupiter as the supreme god; the others, who were bent upon riches, happiness, or pleasure, and a life of ease, Hercules, Mercury, Venus or others; women with child, Diana or Lucina, and so on; thus every one made that his god to which his heart was inclined, so that even in the mind of the heathen to have a god means to trust and believe. But their error is this that their trust is false and wrong for it is not placed in the only God, besides whom there is truly no God in heaven or upon earth. Therefore the heathen really make their self-invented notions and dreams of God an idol, and put their trust in that which is altogether nothing. Thus it is with all idolatry; for it consists not merely in erecting an image and worshiping it, but rather in the heart, which stands gaping at something else, and

---

23. See G. K. Beale, *We Become What We Worship: A Biblical Theology of Idolatry* (Downers Grove, IL: IVP Academic, 2008).
24. Christopher J. H. Wright, *The Mission of God* (Downers Grover, IL: IVP Academic, 2006), 164-5.

seeks help and consolation from creatures, saints, or devils, and neither cares for God, nor looks to Him for so much good as to believe that He is willing to help, neither believes that whatever good it experiences comes from God.

Besides, there is also a false worship and extreme idolatry, which we have hitherto practiced, and is still prevalent in the world, upon which also all ecclesiastical orders are founded, and which concerns the conscience alone that seeks in its own works help, consolation, and salvation, presumes to wrest heaven from God, and reckons how many bequests it has made, how often it has fasted, celebrated Mass, etc. Upon such things it depends, and of them boasts, as though unwilling to receive anything from God as a gift, but desires itself to earn or merit it superabundantly, just as though He must serve us and were our debtor, and we His liege lords. What is this but reducing God to an idol, yea, [a fig image or] an apple-god, and elevating and regarding ourselves as God? But this is slightly too subtle, and is not for young pupils.[25]

Both Wright and Luther describe what happened to Israel in Amos' day. All of their religious activities and idolatry were done to establish their own authority and at the same time use the Lord God for their own ends.

One must not miss the irony of what will happen to Israel with their gods. Many ancient cults had grand processions where the people carried images of their gods up high so all could see. Amos indicates there will be a procession, but it will differ from the ones Israel has been practicing. It will be a procession where their gods lead Israel into exile.[26] It will be the Lord who is the God of hosts, of all the heavenly hosts, who will send Israel into exile along with their astral gods.

One day, I was wearing an outfit like many golfers wear— my shirt even had the PGA (Professional Golfers' Association) logo. A gentleman noticed the logo and asked me if I was a golfer. I said, 'Not really, I just like wearing the clothes they wear.' I wonder if that might not be the case with some when it comes to the family of God. In truth, they may have never really confessed their sin and turned away from that sin and

---

25. Martin Luther, 'The Large Catechism,' in *Triglot Concordia: The Symbolical Books of the Ev. Lutheran Church*, trans. F. Bente and W. H. T. Dau (St. Louis: Concordia Publishing House, 1921), 565.

26. Paul, 197.

trusted in Jesus Christ alone for their salvation, but there are many perks to being associated with the Church: (1) some think religious people are a good, godly people, (2) it is good to associate with truly good and godly people, (3) it is good for one's family as long as they do not become too fanatical about it, and (4) most of the time it makes one feel good about oneself. If one is religious long enough, one might begin to believe that is enough to be right with God. However, no matter how we look or act in our times of corporate worship, if our hearts and lives are not fully committed to the Lordship of Christ and love for His people, we may be deceiving ourselves just as Israel deceived itself. Jesus said,

> Not everyone who says to me, 'Lord, Lord,' will enter the kingdom of heaven, but the one who does the will of my Father who is in heaven. On that day many will say to me, 'Lord, Lord, did we not prophesy in your name, and cast out demons in your name, and do many mighty works in your name?' And then will I declare to them, 'I never knew you; depart from me, you workers of lawlessness.' Everyone then who hears these words of mine and does them will be like a wise man who built his house on the rock. And the rain fell, and the floods came, and the winds blew and beat on that house, but it did not fall, because it had been founded on the rock. And everyone who hears these words of mine and does not do them will be like a foolish man who built his house on the sand. And the rain fell, and the floods came, and the winds blew and beat against that house, and it fell, and great was the fall of it (Matt. 7:21-27).

So would be Israel's impending fall.

Study Questions

1. What leads people to be self-deceived about their relationship to God?

2. How many people today love the idea of following the Lord Jesus Christ without truly loving Him?

3. What did Israel do to demonstrate its religious fervor?

4. Is there possibly a detachment between what people outwardly express in worship and its significance today as it was in Amos' day?

5. How does worship become more about the worshipper and less about God?

6. What is a god?

7. How does self-confidence become a snare to believers?

8

The Peril of Complacency
(Amos 6:1-7)

According to The Road Information Program in the United States, traffic fatalities are occurring on the nation's rural roads at a rate approximately two-and-a-half times higher than on all other roads, even though rural roads carry less than half of America's traffic. Drivers attempting to pass other vehicles on two-lane roads and the inherent dangers of intersections are not the main causes of these fatal accidents. There appear to be two main causes for the majority of these fatalities. First, the construction of rural roads seems to have less stringent safety standards than the construction of highways in urban areas. Second, drivers on rural roads fail to recognize dangers on the road. The lack of apparent danger with less traffic on rural roads seems to be a factor in a number of fatalities because people become more relaxed and take higher risks. Whereas drivers in large cities tend to be more alert because of the obvious potential dangers of other vehicles and road construction, drivers out on country roads often allow the peaceful setting of rural life to dull their senses to the dangers of the road. The problem is drivers often become complacent. According to the Merriam-Webster's Dictionary, complacency is 'self-satisfaction especially when accompanied by unawareness of actual dangers or deficiencies'.[1]

---

1. Accessed 18 January 2010; available from http://www.merriam-webster.com/dictionary/complacency; Internet.

In Amos 6:1-7, Amos describes a people who had become dangerously complacent in his day. Israel's own self-satisfaction and arrogance led to a disbelief of actual impending danger and to unawareness that it was their deficiencies that were causing it. The passage describes how Israel became complacent and serves as warning to believers today. It shows how complacency can become a very real threat to the people of God.

Complacency becomes a threat when we begin to think we are invulnerable (6:1-2)
The men whom Amos addressed were at ease, self-confident and carefree because they felt safe from any harm. They believed themselves to be economically, militarily, and spiritually secure as they looked to Jerusalem on Mount Zion and to Israel's capital on the mountain of Samaria. These great cities served as their financial centers, as their greatest fortified cities, and as symbols of divine blessing and protection. The people believed themselves to be invulnerable.

History is wrought with people who thought themselves to be invulnerable. One such example comes from the Scottish Wars of Independence. At the Battle of Stirling Bridge on September 11, 1297, English noblemen John de Warenne, the 7th Earl of Surrey, and Hugh de Cressingham led their formidable forces of well-trained infantry and heavy cavalry across the Stirling Bridge two-by-two against a greatly outnumbered and 'untrained' Scottish infantry led by Andrew Moray and William Wallace. The English had defeated the Scots many times before, and up to this point no infantry alone had ever been successful in defeating the English heavy cavalry. The English leadership believed the Scottish rabble presented no real danger or threat of defeat, but at the end of the day seventy to ninety percent of the English troops lay dead while the Scots lost very few of their soldiers in the battle. Hugh de Cressingham died in the battle and according to legend the Scots flayed the English nobleman just as his actions against Scotland had flayed their people, and Wallace made a sword belt out of his skin. Their belief in their invulnerability made them complacent and ultimately led to their destruction.

Amos 6:1-7

The writer of Proverbs says, 'Pride goes before destruction, and a haughty spirit before a fall' (16:18). Amos' point was clear. Israel's pride made them believe they were invulnerable, but their destruction was imminent. Why? Because they trusted in what God had given them as opposed to the God who had been so giving to them. The object of their faith had moved from the one true God to what He had provided. What's more, they began to take credit for God's provision. This development in Israel's day raises a question for us: 'Are we trusting in the material things God has given us for security or is our faith centered upon the Lord God Himself?' Jesus taught that we should not be anxious about what we wear or eat or about our futures, but that we should seek first His kingdom as He provides for all our needs. Moreover, He who spared not His own Son but delivered Him up for us all, how will He not freely through Him give us all things? There is the life where one proudly thinks oneself invulnerable that leads to destruction, and there is the life where one humbly recognizes one's weakness but is made strong through faith in the Lord Jesus Christ. As Paul says, 'Therefore, let anyone who thinks that he stands take heed lest he fall' (1 Cor. 10:12).

Complacency becomes a threat when we begin to think we are better than others (6:1-3)
The wealthy noblemen of Israel had become so self-absorbed that they believed themselves to be better than others. Perhaps this attitude provides some explanation of their treatment of the poor. It seems they were wealthy because they believed they deserved to be materially blessed by God, while those less wealthy must have been less worthy of God's blessings. To support such thinking they looked to their powerful positions in Israelite society. All of the people of Israel came to them for judgments and wisdom. Why would the people be looking to them for direction if they were not the best of the nation? Their position and popularity fed their egos.

Position, power, prosperity, and popularity are all possible stumbling blocks that may lead to an attitude of self-importance. The chiming of well-intentioned accolades and the presence of devoted groupies can become quite intoxicating. Unfortunately, many leaders among the people of God fall prey to pride because of such allurements. Many come into their positions of leadership with a desire to serve the Lord and others, but over time they begin expecting others and even the Lord to be their servants. As their sense of superiority increases, their concern for others decreases. Their self-centered will overshadows the needs of the people to whom God called them to serve. Like the people in Amos' time, they literally become 'carefree' when it comes to others. Their attitude of superiority grows as people come to them for godly advice, instruction, and blessing. Leaders in the Church must continually beware of the temptation that may accompany the God-given position and responsibilities inherent in leading God's people. Human depravity ensures no person is safe from such temptations.

Not only did they believe themselves to be the best in the nation, they believed their nation was better than all other nations. In verse two, Amos mentions three other nations: Calneh, Hamath, and Gath of the Philistines. While there is debate as to the exact location of Calneh, many scholars speculate it was located north of Israel on the northern part of the Orontes River.[2] Hamath was located in this same vicinity on the southern part of the Orontes River but still north of Israel. Gath was located on the north-eastern border of Judah very near to the border between Israel and Judah. The city of Hamath was an Aramean state, and the Arameans were long-time enemies of Israel since the time of David. Whenever they were not under Israelite control they were a threat to Israel. Given Calneh was located in the same region dominated by the Arameans and was in the vicinity of Hamath, it is reasonable to suppose it too posed a threat to Israel. Although David broke the five-city coalition that once posed a threat to Israel's very existence, the Philistines continued to engage in conflict with Israel and Judah from time to time.[3] All three of these states apparently posed a threat to Israel's national security not long before Amos began his ministry. King Jeroboam II brought Hamath into submission near the beginning of his

---

2. R. K. Harrison, 'Calneh,' in *The International Standard Bible Encyclopedia*, ed. Geoffrey W. Bromiley, rev. ed. *[ISBE]* (Grand Rapids: Eerdmans, 1979), 1:582.

3. David M. Howard, 'Philistines,' in *Peoples of the Old Testament World*, eds. Alfred J. Hoerth, Gerald L. Mattingly, and Edwin M. Yamauchi (Grand Rapids: Baker Books, 1994), 241.

Amos 6:1-7

reign in Israel (2 Kings 14:28), and it is logical to suppose that as a result Calneh too was no longer a threat to Israel and quite possibly under Israel's submission as well.[4] Early in his reign, King Uzziah of Judah subjugated the Philistines including Gath (2 Chron. 26:6-7). Israel and Judah's victories over these enemies apparently contributed to their air of superiority.[5] They ascribed their victories to themselves and forgot that it was the Lord who had given them (2 Kings 14:25-26). They thought themselves invulnerable. However, according to verse three, the smugness that came as a result of their ability to put off 'the day of disaster' at the hands of these enemies only brought upon them the violence of a far greater enemy, the Lord Himself.

If they are not careful, people in the Church can begin to think they are better than others. Years ago when I was a teenager, my father and I visited a church that was in search of a pastor. This church was the largest of its denomination in that particular state of the USA. When my father asked a leader how the church's search for a pastor was going, the man proceeded to wax eloquently about how great his church was, how it was a cut above other churches, and that they were going to get a pastor that was superior to others. I remember how, even as a boy, I was utterly disgusted by his arrogance. It is a shame, but the last I heard, the church was in serious trouble with a number of issues and was again looking for a pastor after having had problems with previous leadership. The people of God are the people of God by the grace of God. The only thing good about us is Christ in us. Apart from Christ we are no better than anyone else. Apart from Christ we are all condemned. Such an understanding should produce sincere humility toward God and others along with a deep sense of gratitude for God's kindness toward us.

Complacency becomes a threat when our affluence leads us to be so consumed with ourselves that we have no concern for others (6:4-7).

Once Amos had addressed the arrogant attitudes of Israel's leaders, he turned his attention to their decadent deeds. These indulgent people enjoyed feasts stretched out and sprawled

---
4. Garrett, 182.
5. Ibid., 182.

upon their comfortable couches and extravagant beds inlaid with ivory. Just such a bed was later a gift from King Hezekiah of Judah to the Assyrian king, Sennacherib.[6] The menu of their feasts included the most expensive meats of tender cuts of lamb and beef. Their dining was accompanied by music they likened to David's own musical giftedness. Their feasts involved such excessive drinking that they used large sacred vessels instead of goblets in order to guzzle down their wine.[7] They anointed themselves with the finest of oils. The anointing of oneself with oil mixed with perfumes, as it was rubbed into the hair and skin many times, was associated with the best luxuries and pleasures of life.[8]

Here, Amos describes in great detail activity much like a Canaanite religious feast called a *marzēaḥ* given by the god El to his divine assembly.[9] During this feast the gods overate and drank until they were completely full and intoxicated. El became delirious and envisioned a creature with horns and a tail. At the end of the feast, El passed out in his own excrement and urine.[10] This feast was part of Canaanite religious practice. Marvin H. Pope says:

> From the various strands of information, we gather that the *marzēaḥ* was a social and religious institution which included families, owned property, homes for meetings and vineyards for wine supply, was associated with specific deities, and met periodically, perhaps monthly, to celebrate for several days at a stretch with food and drink and sometimes, if not regularly, with sexual orgies.[11]

Amos' description follows the pattern of the Canaanite feast.[12] Apparently, Israel had incorporated the perverse and self-indulgent practices of the Canaanites into their own 'worship'

---

6. D. D. Luckenbill, *The Annals of Sennacherib* (OIP 2; Chicago: University of Chicago, 1924), 34 iii 43.
7. Paul, 208.
8. See Proverbs 21:17; Ecclesiastes 9:7-8; Song of Songs 1:3; Esther 2:12.
9. Max E. Polley, *Amos and the Davidic Empire* (New York: Oxford University Press, 1989), 88.
10. Marvin H. Pope, 'A Divine Banquet at Ugarit,' in *The Use of the Old Testament in the New and Other Essays*, ed. James M. Efird (Durham, NC: Duke University Press, 1972), 170-203.
11. Ibid., 193.
12. Philip J. King, *Amos, Hosea, Micah—An Archaeological Commentary* (Philadelphia: Westminster Press, 1988), 138.

of Yahweh. This display is just another instance where their worship was centered upon themselves not the Lord God. So-called expressions of worship to the Lord were really about self-gratification.

Study Questions

1. What are causes of complacency among God's people?
2. How did Israel develop a sense of invulnerability? Can this be a problem for Christians today?
3. How does a sense of invulnerability become a problem for the people of God?
4. What were the stumbling blocks that led to Israel's arrogance?
5. What are possible stumbling blocks that may lead believers to an attitude of self-importance today?
6. How did affluence become a problem for Israel? How much of a problem does it present to Christians today?
7. When is religious extravagance unacceptable to God?

9

The Fall of the Proud
(Amos 6:8-14)

In *Mere Christianity* C. S. Lewis writes,

> There is one vice of which no man in the world is free; which everyone in the world loathes when he sees it in someone else; and of which hardly any people, except Christians, ever imagine that they are guilty themselves. I have heard people admit that they are bad-tempered, or that they cannot keep their heads about girls or drink, or even that they are cowards. I do not think I have ever heard anyone who was not a Christian accuse himself of this vice. And at the same time I have very seldom met anyone, who was not a Christian, who showed the slightest mercy to it in others. There is no fault which makes a man more unpopular, and no fault which we are more unconscious of in ourselves. And the more we have it ourselves, the more we dislike it in others.... The vice I am talking of is Pride or Self-Conceit.... Pride leads to every other vice: it is the complete anti-God state of mind.[1]

As Lewis observes, many of us have difficulty even imagining we might be guilty of pride or self-conceit. Then again, we might ask ourselves how we feel when someone snubs us, when someone refuses to take notice of us, when someone is showing off, when someone patronizes us, when someone devalues our efforts, or when someone fails miserably in an

---
1. C. S. Lewis, *Mere Christianity*, rev. (New York: Collier Books, 1960), 108-9.

area of life we have not.[2] If we are honest, it will not take most of us long to recognize pride and self-conceit lurking in our hearts and minds.

My oldest son is a senior in high school, and he is presently studying British literature. Every week his teacher requires him to write a review of what he has been reading. A part of the requirement for the review is for the student to have a parent edit the review, so that when he turns in the assignment he must give her his edited first draft and his corrected final draft. Usually, I am the one who edits his work. His teacher has the reputation of being highly skilled and demanding. Her students learn how to write well, and usually do quite well when they go to college. When he received the grade for his first assignment with her, I told my son to call me and let me know what it was. He called me and said 'we' got a 38 out of 40. 'We' failed to put the title in italics. Unknowingly, he threw down the gauntlet. Having been in school for most of my life, I am very driven to excel in the classroom. Since then, I have continued to ask him how 'he' is doing in the class, more so than I have ever done for any of his other classes. The other day I asked if his teacher knows who is editing his papers. My wife overheard and sarcastically said, 'Yes, has the teacher ever called you to her desk and asked you, "Who is your tremendous editor? I am very impressed!"' My son said, 'Dad, you can use that as an illustration on pride.' He was right. What I wanted was recognition; that is pride. You may be thinking this guy really has a problem; I am glad I am not like that. That too is pride.

The Scriptures contain harsh language to convey the Lord's disdain for misplaced pride. For instance:

> God opposes the proud, but gives grace to the humble (James 4:6).

> The LORD preserves the faithful but abundantly repays the one who acts in pride (Ps. 31:23).

> When pride comes, then comes disgrace (Prov. 11:2).

> The LORD tears down the house of the proud (Prov. 15:25).

> Pride goes before destruction, and a haughty spirit before a fall (Prov. 16:18).

---

2. Ibid., 109.

Before destruction a man's heart is haughty, but humility comes before honor (Prov. 18:12).

One's pride will bring him low, but he who is lowly in spirit will obtain honor (Prov. 29:23).

I will put an end to the pomp of the arrogant (Isa. 13:11).

The horror you inspire has deceived you, and the pride of your heart, you who live in the clefts of the rock, who hold the height of the hill. Though you make your nest as high as the eagle's, I will bring you down from there, declares the LORD (Jer. 49:16).

For everyone who exalts himself will be humbled, and he who humbles himself will be exalted (Luke 14:11).

These verses are just a sampling of the numerous passages in the Scriptures that condemn pride. But why is God so opposed to pride? It is because wrongful pride is in opposition to God. The Hebrew scribe, Ben Sira, aptly wrote, 'The beginning of pride is when one departeth from God, and his heart is turned away from his Maker. For pride is the beginning of sin, and he that hath it shall pour out abomination.'[3] In fact, one is never more like Satan than when one becomes full of pride in oneself, for it was his pride that led him to rebel against God. It is pride that led Adam and Eve to sin against God because they believed that if they ate the fruit of the knowledge of good and evil they would be like God. Humility is depending on God; pride is depending on oneself. In a sense, pride is a kind of idolatry. If idolatry involves putting something into God's rightful place, then pride certainly is idolatry. It is when one gives oneself credit when the only credit belongs to God. Instead of recognizing every good gift comes from above, one believes every good gift comes from one's own self-effort. Moreover, such pride is thievery because it seeks to steal God's glory in what He has done.

Imagine attending a ceremony at the White House. On the platform stands the President of the United States of America alongside three soldiers. Next to the president is a stand that has three medals on it. They are all Congressional Medals of Honor. Obviously, you are in attendance at a ceremony where three soldiers will receive this highest of honors in the United

---

3. Ecclesiasticus 10:12-13

States military. These soldiers risked their lives in order to save the lives of numerous comrades in arms. Sitting next to you is a young soldier who has just been drafted into the army. He is not even a volunteer. He has only been in a few days and has hardly gotten used to his new hairstyle or broken in his new uniform. As the ceremony begins, all of a sudden, this young soldier sitting next to you stands and approaches the platform. He walks up to the stand with the three medals, picks one up and puts it on himself. Imagine the travesty of such an act by one who did not even volunteer to serve his country, doing such a thing in light of the tremendous valor and sacrifice depicted by the other three deserving soldiers. He has no right to such a sacred honor. Pride is like that. It is assuming credit and honor for oneself when it rightfully belongs to another, the Lord God.

In Amos 6:8-14, the Lord declares His judgment upon Israel because of her pride. The Lord begins His pronouncement by making the most solemn oath possible; He solemnly swears 'by himself.' All that the Lord is stands behind this proclamation. There can be nothing more certain nor more serious than what the Lord is about to say. The people, then, hear the following words, 'I abhor the pride of Jacob and hate his strongholds, and I will deliver up the city and all that is in it.' The tragedy is that 'the pride of Jacob' had changed. There had been a day when Israel sung of the pride of Jacob as being the inheritance their great king over all the earth had bestowed upon His people, Israel. It was an appropriate pride in their God who had fought for them and established His covenant with them (Ps. 47). Not all pride is sin. The pride and boasting that focuses on the Lord is right and good. The people could sing of His deliverance from their enemies and expect the Lord to protect them in the future because he was the object of their pride. Nevertheless, the object of their pride has now moved away from the Lord and His mighty deeds to themselves and their own handiwork. They believe they are the reason for their own economic prosperity and military superiority. Israel failed to remember Moses' warning about taking credit for what God has done.[4] Therefore, the Lord proclaims He

---

4. See Deuteronomy 6:10-12.

is going to remove that which has become a source of pride for His people. The remainder of this declaration reveals the devastating consequences of wrongful pride or self-conceit.

Wrongful pride will ultimately result in death (6:9-10)
The Lord paints the picture of ten men hiding in a house hoping to escape the ominous instrument of God's judgment. The word 'remain' gives the impression that an initial onslaught against Israel's awesome fortifications will have already occurred and that the ten believe there might be some hope of survival. Maybe they will live to fight another day. However, the Lord's curt statement cuts to the heart as He says, 'they shall die.' There will be no escape. Furthermore, as two relatives come to prepare the corpses for burial, one will ask, 'Are there any more with you?' The other will respond, 'No, and be quiet. We must not mention the Lord's name.' Why must they be careful not to mention the Lord's name? It may be for fear the Lord might bring further calamity.[5] It could be that the land will be so defiled the Lord will not answer.[6] In fact, His judgment will be His answer to their hypocritical calls of worship they are raising in the present. It could be they will not want to mention the Lord's name because He is the cause of the calamity in the first place.[7] What use would it be to call for His blessing now? Or, it may be too late to pray for the Lord's deliverance, because all of the soldiers are dead.[8] Another possibility is that the carnage will be so overwhelming that there will be nothing left to say. All of these factors taken together will be too much. God will speak, and who will be able to answer? The people who boast in themselves will be silenced.

Wrongful pride will ultimately result in total destruction (6:11)
All of the massive fortifications as well as the smallest buildings will be smashed to pieces when the Lord's judgment strikes Israel. This great wreckage will happen at the Lord's command. The objects of Israel's pride will be no more. The

---

5. Paul, 213.
6. Garrett, 196.
7. Anderson and Freedman, 573-4.
8. Smith, *Amos*, 281.

people will finally realize how thoroughly impotent they had been and still are, and how omnipotent the Lord God truly is. The Lord is committed to teaching Israel this truth, no matter what it takes for her to get the message. The same is true with us. Whatever monuments we build, whether physically or figuratively, for our own reputation and glory will end up as rubble. Such building projects are a waste of time and energy. Only what is done for Christ will last.

Wrongful pride results in poor judgment (6:12)
Amos, the farmer and expert in animal husbandry, utilizes questions readily understood in an agrarian culture to make his point. A horse has enough sense to avoid running on treacherous, rocky mountainous terrain. To do so would be to ruin its hooves or to risk injury and possibly risk its life. Furthermore, a farmer knows better than to try to plow such ground. His labors would be unproductive, once again risking injury to his oxen and damage to his plow. Such behavior for a horse or a farmer would be illogical and ridiculous. It does not take a genius to figure this out. What is Amos' point? Anyone who has enough sense to understand how foolish it would be for a horse or a farmer to attempt these things should have enough sense to realize the foolishness of turning 'justice into poison and the fruit of righteousness into wormwood.'

Nonetheless, Israel has so perverted her system of justice and her standards of what is right and wrong that Israelite society became just as dangerous to the people as rocky terrain was to a horse or to a farmer's oxen. The people turned away from God and turned on one another. They failed to realize all of it would implode on them, causing them great harm. Israel's pride caused them to ignore the severe consequences their actions would bring. Israel's pride caused them to ignore God. The psalmist says, 'In the pride of his face the wicked does not seek him; all his thoughts are, "There is no God"' (Ps. 10:4). Because of our sinful nature, if we believe we can do without God, we will. However, to do so is foolishness. The Bible says, 'Do you see a man who is wise in his own eyes? There is more hope for a fool than for him' (Prov. 26:12). To believe our ways are better than God's ways and to think we know more than what God knows is pure insanity. A self-conceited heart leads to disgrace, but one who humbly depends on God is wise (Prov. 2:10). Certainly, Israel had become a disgrace. Instead of being a light to the nations, shining the glory of God abroad, the nations witnessed a pompous people, who in the end were nothing worthy of note.

Wrongful pride results in delusional thinking (6:13)
Not only has Israel's pride and self-conceit led to poor judgment, but also it has caused the people to be delusional in their thinking. They believed their military victories were the result of their own fighting prowess and strength under the leadership of Jeroboam II and not because God granted them their victories. They took credit for what God had done for them. The first place Amos mentions is called Lo-debar. It was located east of the Jordan River in the territory of the Ammonites in northern Gilead.[9] Amos' mention of Lo-debar is ironic. Lo-debar literally means 'nothing.' Therefore, their rejoicing about their victory over the fall of Lo-debar is actually rejoicing about defeating 'nothing.' The second city is Karnaim. Its name literally means 'two horns', and it was located in Aram.[10] It was a relatively insignificant city.[11] Amos quotes the people as they boasted about their taking this city by their own strength for themselves, but wrongful pride will result in such delusional thinking. They were proud of conquering 'two horns.' Now that is something about which to brag.

We need to ask ourselves, 'What can we accomplish apart from the Lord?' Jesus said, 'Apart from me you can do nothing' (John 15:5). Everything we are or are able to do is because of the Lord, who is our Creator. What's more, He often intervenes on our behalf more than we can realize. Jimmy Stewart's character in *Shenandoah* illustrates an attitude of pride. As his family bows to pray and give thanks for the food before they eat supper, he says something like this, 'Lord, thank you for this food even though *we* plowed the fields by the sweat of our brows, even though *we* planted the seed under the hot

---
9. Briscoe, 135.
10. Ibid.
11. B. Smith, 123.

sun, even though *we* picked the corn and the beans, even though *we* prepared this food. Thanks anyway.' This fictional character has failed to realize it is the Lord who provided him with the land, with the sun and the rain, with a body and mind able to do the work, and with a family that helped him. All of these things and more come from God in real life.

Wrongful pride results in total devastation (6:14)
As powerful as Israel believed and boasted her army to be, it did not compare to 'The Lord of Hosts' or 'The Lord of the Armies.' The Lord will raise an army from a nation against Israel so massive that all of Israel will be oppressed by it, from Israel's northernmost boundary in Lebo-Hamath to Israel's southernmost boundary at the Brook of the Arabah. None will escape the reach of this army. Although from history we know it was Assyria that God used as His instrument of judgment, the Lord does not reveal to Israel what nation it will be who comes against her. Surely, this ambiguity heightened the mystery and ominous nature of the Lord's declaration. On the other hand, the people may have scoffed at the Lord's prophet, proudly thinking he could not even mention a nation that could pose such a threat. Whatever the case, within thirty to forty years Israel would discover what Amos was saying was true.

The apostle Paul says pride exalts itself against the knowledge of God (2 Cor. 10:5). Therefore, in order for the people of God to know Him and to walk in His ways we must recognize who He is and, in that light, who we are. He is the creator; it is He who has made us and not we ourselves (Ps. 100:3).[12] No matter how much we desire to be in control and our sinful nature leads us to think we can be like God, we cannot. Not long after my wife and I were married, we got a dog. He was an Australian shepherd mix, and we named him Goliath. For some reason, Goliath made me the center of his universe. When I came home, he greeted me at the door. When I told him to sit, he would sit. Wherever I walked in the house, he followed me to the left and a few inches behind. I was his god, and I loved it. I wondered what life would be like if everything

---

12. King James Version.

else went my way as it was with Goliath. Like Adam and Eve, we all have in us a desire to be like God. However, when we give in to this desire we fail to think clearly, we become delusional, and we ultimately experience devastating loss, the most devastating being sweet fellowship with the Lord who loved us, called us, and saved us from eternal judgment.

STUDY QUESTIONS

1. Why is the conceit of God's people so reprehensible to God?
2. Why are people so susceptible to pride?
3. What source of pride is appropriate for the people of God?
4. According to Amos, what is it God abhors?
5. What will result from the wrongful pride of God's people?
6. How is conceit foolish?
7. How does pride lead to delusional thinking?

10

Judgment, Intercession, and Mercy
(Amos 7:1-9)

Amos 7 begins another major section of the book. It contains five visions Amos receives from the Lord (7:1-3; 4-6; 7-9; 8:1-3; 9:1-4). The first two visions are alike in that they are event visions, describing a catastrophic event God will bring upon Israel. The second two visions are wordplay visions employing symbolism to convey their message, and the fifth vision is distinct in its form and content, showing the Lord executing His judgment upon Israel.[1] The five visions present a unified message of the Lord God's intention to carry out His judgment upon Israel. However, the visions demonstrate a progression also. In the first two visions, Amos is overtaken by the severity of the Lord's judgment and pleads with the Lord to forgive the people and relent of the judgment. Upon seeing the next pair of visions, Amos is moved to compassion, but his request is for the Lord to relent with no mention of God's forgiving the people. In the fifth vision, Amos has no response whatsoever. It appears as the visions continue, Amos realizes the overwhelming guilt of Israel and the determination of God to judge His people for their rebellion.

Furthermore, it is interesting to note the first four visions appear in pairs. The repetition of these visions in form and intent confirms the magnitude of their message and validates

---

1. B. Smith, 126.

their authenticity. With each pair, the Lord communicates the same message in two different visions. He did this previously with Joseph and the Pharaoh Joseph served. Joseph had two visions: one involved sheaves and the sun, and the second contained the moon and eleven stars. Both visions communicated the same message concerning the future of Joseph and his brothers. The Pharaoh had two visions: the first was of two sets of seven cows, and the second of two sets of ears of grain. These two visions also communicated the same message of seven years of plenty followed by seven years of famine. Joseph makes this clear when he says, 'The dreams of Pharaoh are one; God has revealed to Pharaoh what he is about to do' (Gen. 41:25). Joseph also declares the purpose of these pairing of visions saying, 'And the doubling of Pharaoh's dream means that the thing is fixed by God, and God will shortly bring it about' (Gen. 41:32).[2] The doubling of Amos' visions appears to function in the same way.

A vision of swarming locusts (7:1-3)
Amos' first vision is of the Lord's forming a swarm of locusts to come upon Israel.[3] The vision is very clear as to the timing of this calamity. It is to come after the king has gotten the first share of the harvest but before the people have the opportunity to get their share of it. This practice was probably some form of tax. If so, the king's portion may have been expansive if it was what he used to provide for his government officials and sizeable military machine. The late spring crop or second crop comes with the late spring rains of March to April and the promise of spring. This second crop consisted of non-grain crops such as vegetables. The timing of the swarm of locusts will be especially devastating to the entire nation. It is a time when the second crop is just beginning and the first crop of grain is already well on its way to being ready for harvest. Therefore, the swarm will not only destroy the 'second crop' consisting of the vegetables, but it will destroy the nation's unharvested first crop of grain too. The people's survival will

---

2. Paul, 224.
3. For locusts, see Y. Palmoni, 'Locust,' *The Interpreter's Dictionary of the Bible* (Nashville: Abingdon, 1962), 3:144-8; also see the discussion of Amos 4:9.

be in question with such an ill-timed blow.[4] With the oncoming dry season of summer, the people will be left destitute with little remaining to feed themselves or their livestock. A people who have become self-reliant will discover just how utterly dependent upon their Creator they really are for provision and sustenance.

Amos was overwhelmed by this vision and its devastation upon the people, and with good reason. According to *National Geographic*,

> Locust swarms devastate crops and cause major agricultural damage and attendant human misery—famine and starvation. They occur in many parts of the world, but today locusts are most destructive in sustenance farming regions of Africa. The desert locust is notorious. Found in Africa, the Middle East, and Asia, they inhabit some 60 countries and can cover one-fifth of Earth's land surface. Desert locust plagues may threaten the economic livelihood of one-tenth of the world's humans. A desert locust swarm can be 460 square miles (1,200 square kilometres) in size and pack between 40 and 80 million locusts into less than half a square mile (one square kilometre). Each locust can eat its weight in plants each day, so a swarm of such size would eat 423 million pounds (192 million kilograms) of plants every day. Like the individual animals within them, locust swarms are typically in motion and can cover vast distances. In 1954, a swarm flew from northwest Africa to Great Britain. In 1988, another made the lengthy trek from West Africa to the Caribbean.[5]

The vision concludes with all of Israel's vegetation being devoured by the locusts. This vision is much like what Egypt experienced when the Lord sent locusts upon that land. Israel's sin had become so great they were deserving of the same punishment their taskmasters received (Exod. 10:12). Oppressors will experience the judgment of God no matter who they are. It is difficult to imagine the depth of the devastation Amos witnessed in this vision, but it was so dreadful he pled on Israel's behalf for the Lord to pardon the nation.

While people think of the role of the prophet as one who represents God to the people, many fail to realize the role of the

---

4. Paul, 227.
5. See *National Geographic* [on-line]; accessed 10 November 2009; available from http://animals.nationalgeographic.com/animals/bugs/locust.html; Internet.

prophet was also to mediate on behalf of others, especially the people of God.[6] Speaking to Abimelech concerning Abraham the Lord said, 'He is a prophet, and he will pray for you, and you shall live' (Gen. 20:7). Abraham also interceded for Sodom (Gen. 18:23-33). Early in Israel's history Moses demonstrated his concern for God's people through intercessory prayer (Num. 14:11-14, 31-32). Samuel also interceded for God's people when the people suffered (1 Sam. 7:5-13) or turned away from God's will (1 Sam. 12:18-23). It is the prophet's responsibility to stand in the breach when God's people are in harm's way (Ezek. 13:4-5; 22:30). Like prophets who came before him, Amos interceded for the people, hoping God would relent of His plans for Israel. Amos' request was not for forgiveness based upon Israel's repentance; it was a request for Israel's complete pardon based only upon God's mercy and grace. Through Moses the Lord said, 'The LORD, the LORD, a God merciful and gracious, slow to anger, and abounding in steadfast love and faithfulness, keeping steadfast love for thousands, forgiving iniquity and transgression and sin' (Exod. 34:6-7). There is no question Israel deserved the Lord's discipline, and there is no doubt Amos suffered opposition from the people as demonstrated by Amaziah the priest (7:12-13).

Nonetheless, Amos cared about the people to whom the Lord called him to minister. Therefore, he called upon God's tender mercies to save the people. Such compassion reflects a true godliness that leaders need to exhibit in the church today. Because of our negligence most pray very little for those to whom God has given us to minister. How much more difficult is it to pray on behalf of those who oppose us as we serve the Lord? If we do remember them in prayer we are tempted to pray for God's judgment upon them rather than God's mercy and pardon. Amos' concern reflects the heart of the Lord Jesus Christ for Israel when he said, 'O Jerusalem, Jerusalem, the city that kills the prophets and stones those who are sent to it! How often would I have gathered your children together as a hen gathers her brood under her wings, and you would not! See, your house is left to you desolate' (Matt. 23:37-8). The desire is for an intimacy between God and His people.

---

6. See Michael J. Williams, *The Prophet and His Message* (Phillipsburg, NJ: P & R Publishing, 2003), 88-90.

Amos' request for the Lord's pardon was based upon the fact that Israel could not survive because she was so small. Obviously, Israel did not think of herself as small, but Amos was not describing the nation in light of its own perspective but in light of God's perspective, which is the only true perspective. Compared to others, Israel thought of herself as first among nations, yet in comparison to God the nation was impotent. If only the people had recognized that for themselves. Instead, the Lord intends to enlighten them to this truth.

James says, 'The prayer of a righteous person has great power as it is working' (James 5:16). Such is the case with Amos when he interceded on Israel's behalf. Notice God's response to Amos: 'The LORD relented concerning this; "It shall not be," said the LORD' (7:3). The Lord did not pardon Israel, but He did hold back His judgment, giving Israel more opportunity to repent of her sin against God. He is a patient God. Such action reveals the twofold nature of God in that He is just and therefore must punish sin, but also He is merciful and gracious, ready to forgive the repentant soul. The passage also reveals how God answers the unselfish prayer of His servant.

A vision of a consuming fire (7:4-6)

The second vision is much like the first. Both begin with 'what the Lord God showed' Amos. Both judgments result in the devouring of the land. Amos pleads to the Lord on Israel's behalf after each of the visions, and in both visions the Lord relents of His judgment and declares what was depicted in the vision shall not happen. Again, the repetition in form emphasizes the message of total devastation.

In this vision, Amos sees the Lord calling judgment upon Israel with a fire that will consume the land and the great deep beneath. The nature of this fire is unclear. It could be a molten lava that pours out of the deep upon the earth. Some argue it is a scorching heat that dries up the waters beneath the ground and burns up all vegetation.[7] What is clear is that the Lord is the source of this fire that will consume the great deep and the land of Israel. The results of it will be unbearable for land and creature alike.

---

7. B. Smith, 131; Paul, 231.

Once again, Amos cries out to the Lord on Israel's behalf. Instead of asking the Lord to pardon Israel, this time he asks the Lord to cease what He is doing. And once again, the Lord relents of His judgment. The Lord heard Amos' plea for those deserving of fiery judgment. Amos should be an example to every believer of the importance of passionately praying for those who are heading for God's fiery judgment. Every believer should rejoice in knowing we have a Savior seated at the right hand of God who intercedes for us (Rom. 8:34).[8] Therefore, we demonstrate Christlikeness when we intercede for others. What difference would it make if God's people had the character of Amos to serve the Lord without pretence and the compassion of Amos to intercede for others in need of God's mercy and grace? This passage should remind us of the power of prayer.

How should we understand the statement, 'the Lord relented'? Some translations say the Lord 'repented'. First, we should recognize this word in its original language is almost always used only of the Lord. Therefore, we should be guarded against thinking the Lord may experience some moral change as might happen with a human being. We should allow God's use of the word about Himself to dictate our understanding of it. Second, we need to recognize the Lord uses human language to convey spiritual truths. The biblical writers often portray God in anthropomorphic terms because the only way human beings can conceive of God is in human terminology.[9] In other words, the only way humans can describe things pertaining to God is in human terminology. Therefore, as frail humans, we are limited in our complete understanding of God and His ways.

The word does not mean so much a change of mind but more a change of course. However, even this understanding can be misleading. We should ask some questions as we try to answer the original question. Will God always, ultimately, judge sin? The answer is yes, on the cross for believers and in hell for unbelievers. Is it God's desire to forgive those who truly turn away from their sin and turn to God in repentance

---

8. Niehaus, 454.
9. Honeycutt, 126; see Genesis 2:2; 6:6; Exodus 15:7; 31:18; Deuteronomy 28:63; Psalms 47:8; 106:40; Ezekiel 21:17; Isaiah 7:18.

and faith for the forgiveness of sin? Again, the answer is yes (2 Pet. 3:9; 1 John 1:9). Therefore, God's relenting when it comes to His judgment is no change in God's mind whatsoever. He is consistent in His justice to ultimately punish sin while at the same time being consistent in demonstrating His desire to give people the opportunity to repent of their sin.

Motyer provides great insight concerning God's relenting concerning judgment when he writes:

> The revelation of the locusts and fire is a statement of our deserving—now and always. Equally, it represents a perpetual element in the divine nature: God's ceaseless wrath against sin. We must not think that suddenly God's anger got the better of Him and flared out against His people but that, happily, Amos was on hand to pray Him into a better mind. The wrath of God is perpetual: the automatic reaction of a holy nature faced with rebellion and ungodliness. But equally eternal is His determination to take, save and keep a people for Himself. This is what the Scripture means when it speaks of Jesus as the Lamb slain from the foundation of the world (Rev. 13:8, RV; *cf.* 1 Pet. 1:19, 20) and of Christians as chosen in Him before the foundation of the world (Eph. 1:4). It is because we cannot unify these two revealed strands of the divine nature that the Lord graciously accommodated the truth to our powers of expression and speaks of Himself as 'repenting'. He represents Himself as hearing prayer and turning from wrath to mercy in order that we may thus understand something of what is involved in His love for us and how great is that love when He beholds us in all our need. On the one hand, there must be that in His love which satisfies and soothes His wrath: for the exercise of the one attribute cannot bludgeon the other out of existence, else there were war and not harmony in the divine nature. It has been revealed to us that it is the blood of Jesus, the great divine gift of love, which satisfies the divine wrath (Rom. 3:25). On the other hand, when the Lord looks upon His people mercy triumphs over wrath.[10]

God is a just God who will punish sin; God is a merciful and gracious God who is ready to forgive the one who turns to Him and away from sin through His Son, Jesus Christ. It is of utmost importance that the church proclaim this message today. We must follow Amos' example of courage and stead-

---

10. Motyer, 156-7.

fast faithfulness to proclaim God's Word. With burdened hearts we must be true to God's message of judgment for those who are outside of Christ. The Lord Jesus Christ said, 'The Son of Man will send his angels, and they will gather out of his kingdom all causes of sin and all law-breakers, and throw them into the fiery furnace. In that place there will be weeping and gnashing of teeth' (Matt. 13:41-2). At the same time, we must proclaim the good news of salvation in Christ for those who by faith and repentance come to Him. The Lord Jesus also said: 'For God so loved the world, that he gave his only Son, that whoever believes in him should not perish but have eternal life. For God did not send his Son into the world to condemn the world, but in order that the world might be saved through him' (John 3:16-17). We must be faithful to proclaim God's message of judgment and salvation. Amos' warning means there is still time for the people to repent. Like the thief on the cross who turned to Christ in faith, they still have one last opportunity. Nevertheless, that window of opportunity is closing for Israel as it is closing for all who do not know the Savior. Like the other thief who died beside the Lord discovered, ultimately that window of opportunity will shut, to be opened no more.

A vision of a revealing plumb line (7:7-9)
The third vision reminds me of my days as a young man playing baseball. I was a pitcher and always enjoyed hearing the umpire proclaim, 'Strike three; you're out!' when I was on the mound. On the other hand, I experienced sorrow and disappointment when I heard the umpire say those same words when I was the batter. In this instance, the Lord is the pitcher and Israel is the batter. After the first two visions, the Lord relented of his judgment and Israel had another chance to hit, so to speak. The Lord gave the people another opportunity to repent of their sin. However, in the third vision Israel has struck out. The Lord will withhold his judgment on Israel no longer.

This vision commences with the Lord asking Amos a question, 'Amos, what do you see?' Amos replies, 'A plumb line.' The Hebrew word, translated here as 'plumb line' in most English translations, only occurs in this text in the entire

Old Testament, causing debate as to what it really means. Therefore, a number of biblical scholars have investigated its meaning and have provided a variety of possibilities.[11] Nevertheless, what has become the traditional translation, 'plumb line,' seems to make the most sense, given the context.[12] A plumb line was made of a plummet, which is a stone or metal weight, attached to a cord. Builders used it to measure a wall to see if the wall was vertically straight.[13] In this instance, the Lord is the builder, and He is measuring Israel to see if she meets His approval. Even though the Lord has shown mercy upon His people, He still holds them accountable to the standards of justice and righteousness of His covenant He established with them (5:24).[14] Israel fails the examination miserably (6:12). Like a wall that was once sturdy and straight but now is crooked and in disrepair, so has Israel become. God's people have neglected their calling and the covenant the Lord had made with them. They ceased to be the light to the nations God called them to be and as a result they forfeited His blessings. Therefore, like a wall that is out of line, Israel must be brought down. As the one who built Israel, the Lord has the right to bring her down.

In light of this vision, we should look inside ourselves and see what the plumb line for our lives is. We live in a society where standards of morality vacillate according to the situation and heart's desire. The 'I'm O.K., you're O.K.' generation has taught us each person's standard of morality is valid; however, if you murder someone, see how far this philosophy will take you. The idea in Western society that everyone's standard of morality is valid has been shaken in the face of Islamic terrorists who kill others in the name of their sense of morality. I recall being taught that I have a right to do whatever I please as long as it does not infringe upon the rights of others. This notion is only true if we acknowledge the Lord as one of the 'others'. In fact, He is the only one of the 'others' that really matters because as the Creator He holds

---

11. See Garrett's overview of scholarly conclusions, 212-14.
12. H. G. M. Williamson, 'The Prophet and the Plumb-line: A Redaction-Critical Study of Amos vii,' *Oudtestamentische Studiën* 26 (1990): 121.
13. K. H. Maahs, 'Measuring Line,' in *The International Standard Bible Encyclopedia*, ed. Geoffrey W. Bromiley, rev. ed. (Grand Rapids: Eerdmans, 1986), 3:295.
14. See 5:7 and 6:12 also.

the rights to all of His creation. To sin against another made in the image of God is to sin against God. Believers need to ask themselves how much they have been influenced by the vacillating standards of our day. For in truth, there is only one standard, and it is the standard of God's Word. To live according to any other standard is to live in rebellion against the Lord.

The Lord says, 'I will never again pass by them' (v. 8). This phrase has a couple of connotations. First, it points back to the first two visions where the Lord relented of His judgment upon Israel. He has shown mercy to Israel in the past, but he will show mercy to Israel no more. Second, when the Lord passed by Moses in Exodus 33, it was a sign of God's kindness toward Israel. However, as will be in the days of Isaiah and Jeremiah, Israel has now passed over or overlooked the Lord, His gracious covenant, and standards of justice and righteousness for His people.[15] Therefore, the Lord will overlook His people.

The Lord appears to have three targets in particular for His judgment: the high places of Isaac, the sanctuaries of Israel, and the house of Jeroboam, Israel's king. The Lord will bring down the two social institutions upon which the nation depends the most: Israel's religion and Israel's monarchy.[16] Their reliance upon the faith of their forefathers will come crashing down. Traveling to sacred places in order to commemorate Isaac's submission to the Lord and the Lord's blessing of Isaac cannot protect the people of Israel from the Lord's wrath. Such demonstrations of faith in the past are unable to substitute for Israel's rebellion in the present. People cannot hope to stand before God based upon the faith of their fathers. Each is called into account for his own actions.

Furthermore, the sanctuaries at Bethel and Dan, with their graven images and substitute priesthood, were an abomination to the Lord. These sanctuaries demonstrated how the people disregarded God's instructions on how to worship Him. They should have realized that one comes to God His way or

---

15. See Isaiah 24:5 and Jeremiah 34:18; Elna K. Solvang, 'Amos 7:7-15: Commentary on First Reading' (article prepared for Lectionary July 12, 2009) [online]; accessed 13 November 2009; available from http://www.workingpreacher.org/default.aspx; Internet.
16. G. Smith, *NIV Application*, 368.

not at all. When it comes to the Lord, there is no negotiation. The only way a person can come to God is on His terms. For instance, the Lord Jesus Christ clearly states the only way to the Father is through His Son (John 14:6). Anyone who attempts to come to the Father any other way is as a 'thief and a robber' (John 10:1). It is only through the work of Christ we may come to the Father. No works of our own will suffice to meet God's standard of righteousness. What's more, God's people need to pay attention to how they approach the Lord in worship. If we adopt a 'come just as you are to worship' attitude, our attempts to worship may not be acceptable to God. David asks and answers, 'Who shall ascend the hill of the LORD? And who shall stand in his holy place? He who has clean hands and a pure heart, who does not lift up his soul to what is false and does not swear deceitfully' (Ps. 24:3-4). The Lord is concerned with what we do and what we think as we come to worship Him. The psalmist also says, 'If I regard wickedness in my heart, the Lord will not hear' (Ps. 66:18, NASB). No amount of religious fervor can erase sin in the heart of an individual. The sacrifice of praise will only be acceptable when it comes from the child of God who has 'clean hands and a pure heart.' Otherwise, just as in Amos' day, the Lord will not listen.

Finally, the Lord says, 'I will rise against the house of Jeroboam with the sword' (v. 9). Jeroboam was a sign of Israel's pride and security. Not since the days of Solomon had Israel experienced such prosperity. However, Jeroboam was a wicked king before the Lord. The Lord would hold him responsible for his sins as he led the people further away from God. Leaders in every realm of authority should take note. As a leader, are you teaching those under your authority to depend on you or to depend on the Lord? Are you taking those who follow you to the Savior, or are you leading them astray and ultimately to destruction? Hopefully, like the apostle Paul you can say, 'Finally, brothers, whatever is true, whatever is honorable, whatever is just, whatever is pure, whatever is lovely, whatever is commendable, if there is any excellence, if there is anything worthy of praise, think about these things. What you have learned and received and heard and seen in me—practice these things, and the God of peace will be with you' (Phil. 4:8-9). Jeroboam and Israel were not going to experience the Lord coming in peace; the Lord was coming to wage war.

Study Questions

1. How does God's discipline upon His people communicate their desperate need for God?
2. What do Amos' pleas for God's mercy reveal about God's prophet?
3. What does God's initially relenting of judgment reveal about God?
4. How does a message of judgment demonstrate God's grace?
5. How important is it for one to recognize both God's perpetual hatred of sin and love for sinners?
6. What is significant about God's unwillingness to relent of His judgment upon Israel in the latter visions when He was willing to do so in the first two visions?
7. What is the problem with a 'come just as you are' attitude when it comes to a believer's worship of the Lord?

11

Who's the Boss?
(Amos 7:10-17)

Who's the Boss? was a popular American sitcom from 1984 to 1992. The series centered around Angela, the driven advertising executive, and her son Jonathan, Tony, her live-in housekeeper, and his daughter Samantha, and Mona, Angela's mother. At one point or other each character attempted to be in control of the household's affairs, thus the title to the sitcom. As a result of the three visions of Amos 7, especially the third vision, Amos 7:10-17 addresses this same question.[1] Who is the ultimate authority? It is a question every individual must answer. Also, whenever God's servants are faithful to proclaim His Word, eventually they can expect someone to question their authority. It was true with the Lord Jesus Christ, it was true with the apostle Paul, and it was true with Amos. The confrontation of Amos 7:10-17 addresses the question, 'Who's the boss?'

Is it the king?
Verse 10 introduces Amaziah. The text indicates Amaziah was 'the priest of Bethel,' which probably means he was the chief priest or high priest of Bethel. His tone of authority and direct correspondence to the king suggest as much. Bethel was the location of one of two religious shrines established by King

---
1. B. K. Smith recognizes this question of authority as being the key to understanding Amos 7:10-17 as well, 134-42.

Jeroboam I in the north when Israel and Judah split into two separate monarchies (1 Kings 12:26-33). These shrines in the north were meant to be replacements for worship at the temple in Jerusalem and were an affront to the Lord God. Along with these shrines the king appointed his own priesthood to oversee them. This act also demonstrated a disregard for God's law. What's more, when Jeroboam I established these religious shrines, it was at Bethel and not Dan, the location of the other royal religious shrine in the north, where he dedicated this new religious cult. Therefore, Amaziah's appointment as high priest at Bethel would have been most prestigious and closely associated with the king's authority.

As a reaction to Amos' preaching at Bethel, Amaziah sent a message to King Jeroboam. Amaziah's message to the king was direct. He accused Amos of insurrection and of instigating a conspiracy to remove Jeroboam from the throne. Of course, Amos had in no way asserted this intention. Amos did say that the Lord would put an end to Jeroboam's dynasty. Therefore, Amaziah took creative license in his message and attempted to convince the king that Amos was calling for the king's assassination. This message surely got the king's attention, given the fact his own dynasty came to the throne as the result of a conspiracy incited by the prophet Elisha where Jehu assassinated King Joram and slaughtered all the princes of Joram's dynasty (2 Kings 9–10). Jeroboam witnessed two such coups occur in Judah as well.[2] Amaziah certainly knew what would get the king's attention. Jeroboam died of natural causes (2 Kings 14:29). It was his son, Zechariah, who would be assassinated (2 Kings 15:8-10). Notice how Amaziah said that they were Amos' words and not 'the word of the Lord.' In addition, Amaziah omitted the reason for the message of judgment, Israel's sins against God.[3] Most importantly, Amaziah never mentioned God's call for Israel to return to Him for restoration. Amaziah crafted his message in order to cast Amos in the worst possible light without any concern for Israel's spiritual condition. When we find ourselves in similar situations it would do us well to remember the words of the Lord Jesus Christ when He said, 'Blessed are you when

---

2. See 2 Kings 12:20; 14:19.
3. Paul, 240.

others revile you and persecute you and utter all kinds of evil against you falsely on my account' (Matt. 5:11). Nevertheless, Amaziah was accurate regarding Amos' prediction of exile for the people.[4] The most alluring lies are often mixed with some aspect of truth.

Amaziah's message to Jeroboam also indicates Amos' message was having an effect. This is seen in his saying, 'the land is not able to bear all his words,' and by the mere fact that Amaziah was compelled to write the king concerning Amos. If Amos' ministry had no effect, then Amaziah would have seen no need to address the issue. It could mean Amaziah was complaining about Amos' incessant preaching; it could mean Amos' message was even spilling over into neighboring nations, getting their attention; it could mean Amos was discouraging and frightening the people; or it could mean that Amaziah feared a real insurrection was bubbling up among the people.[5] The text is silent as to how Amos' message was affecting 'the land', but it was such that the leader of the religious establishment had heard enough and wanted Amos to go home. My father grew up on farms in north central Arkansas and southeast Missouri, so I grew up hearing what I often call 'Arkansasisms' from my father, even though I grew up in cities in the northern United States where my father was a pastor. One of these Arkansasisms was, 'If you throw a rock in a chicken pen, the one that squawks is the one you hit.' Amaziah had gotten 'hit' by Amos' 'rock,' and he was squawking to the king and to Amos about it. Whether or not the land could bear no more, it is obvious Amaziah could bear no more. Amaziah had heard enough of Amos' message.

Christians should not be surprised when enemies of the Lord Jesus Christ attempt to use the government to suppress the proclamation of the gospel. They should not be surprised when the government supports these enemies. Israel had once been a glorious place under David's leadership as the nation faithfully worshipped the Lord. In spite of this, it did not take long for Israel's leaders and its people to begin turning away from God. While there are pockets of revival at times in Israel's history, overall it experiences a continued downward

---

4. See Amos 4:2-3; 5:5, 26-27; 6:7; 9:4.
5. Garrett, 219.

spiral away from the Lord. In Jesus' day, the religious leaders used the Roman governor to kill the Lord. If it happened in Israel, it can happen in any nation. Down through history leaders of governments have tried to control the religious affairs of their people. Hitler eliminated those who opposed him in the Church and replaced them with people who were cordial to the Nazi party. The Communists of the former U.S.S.R. had tight control over the Church. The Ayatollah Khomeini established Islam as the national religion of Iran. Early in America's history, colonists contended with government-only sanctioned religion. The governing body of the colony of Massachusetts expelled Roger Williams because of his opposition to a civil-controlled religion, and he fled for his life in the heart of winter. Were it not for native Americans he would not have survived.[6] John Clarke was arrested for leading an unauthorized worship meeting. He paid a fine, but his assistant, Obadiah Holmes, refused to pay the fine and received 30 lashes.[7] Throughout history various governments have aggressively opposed God's work, and one by one these leaders have fallen. Scripture seems to indicate governmental persecution of God's servants will continue until the Lord comes again. We must remember these governments rise and fall at the Lord's bidding. He is the King of kings and Lord of lords.

Is it the religious establishment?

For Amaziah, reporting Amos to the king was not enough. Amaziah took it upon himself to confront Amos. He began by addressing Amos as a 'seer.' This term was often used of prophets in the Old Testament, and while it may have negative connotations, most of the time it does not.[8] Amaziah used this denotation probably in response to the visions Amos saw and revealed just prior to this confrontation. Also, Amos 1:1 indicates his words came from what he saw. Amaziah told Amos to quickly return to Judah, Amos' home. The situation

---

6. H. Leon McBeth, *The Baptist Heritage: Four Centuries of Baptist Witness* (Nashville: Broadman Press, 1987), 127-9.
7. Ibid., 139-40.
8. See 1 Samuel 22:5; 2 Samuel 24:11; 2 Chronicles 21:9; 29:25; 2 Kings 17:13; Isaiah 29:10; 30:10. It is negatively used in Micah 3:7.

is similar to that of Balaam when King Balak told him to return home. Both Balak and Amaziah recognized Balaam and Amos as legitimate prophets, but both were displeased with what came out of the prophets' mouths.[9] Amaziah told Amos to go home and make his living as a prophet there. Amaziah could not care less whether Amos continued to prophesy, but if Amos was going to continue, Amaziah wanted him to do so somewhere else. Amaziah was one of those mentioned by Amos who commanded the prophets to cease prophesying (2:12). In fact, all that Amaziah really accomplished was to authenticate everything Amos had proclaimed about Israel's king and its religious establishment.[10] The plumb line in Amos' vision was accurate.

The reason Amaziah gave for confronting Amos was because he believed Amos was opposing the authority of the king and the authority of Israel's religious establishment. Israel's religious establishment manifested three characteristics.[11] First, it saw itself as responsible to the government and to its own leadership. In its eyes, there were no greater authorities. Second, it favored the status quo and branded any message that upset the status quo, even a message from God, as provocative and conspiratorial. There was no room for correction, even though their religious activities had become substitutes for faithful obedience to God. Therefore, third, there was no place for criticism. Any criticism would be a threat to the very foundation of their religious establishment. Like Amaziah, leaders of religious establishments today often will not listen to any words that might suggest there is a need for change. They too may use intimidating tactics, appealing to their own authority in order to browbeat people into quiet and peaceful submission. In truth, such defensive tactics are an indication something is terribly wrong. It is a sign of pride and weakness. It conveys an attitude that one has 'arrived' and has no need for change. They are no longer teachable, if they ever were in the first place. Also, it demonstrates a fear that the need for change might be exposed. Their philosophy of leadership is to act like they know everything and have all the answers whether they really do

---

9. Paul, 242.
10. Motyer, 169.
11. Honeycutt, 133.

so or not. Like the emperor in Hans Christian Andersen's *The Emperor's New Clothes*, they surround themselves with people who tell them what they want to hear instead of the truth.[12] These leaders like to think they are team players because they surround themselves with so many people, but they have deceived themselves. They eliminate or discount any perceived opposition or critique without weighing its accuracy or benefit. Nonetheless, like the emperor in the story, eventually they too will be exposed.

Amaziah appealed to the authorities of the king and his own position in the religious establishment of Israel for his self-preservation. Amos had made it clear that Israel's religious activities were pointless. If the people were to repent of their sin, it would have a direct impact on the false priesthood leading their worship. Their positions of leadership and authority would be in jeopardy. Amaziah's concern for the king was directly connected to Amaziah's concern for himself. Grasps for power are all too common in the Church and religious institutions. How many pastors have experienced opposition because leaders feared losing their power? How many pastors have been told to quit preaching messages that make people uncomfortable because they are so convicting? How many pastors hold such a tight grip on their congregations that no one else in the congregation may serve and lead in any capacity? Too many times have I witnessed people in the church twist the truth and forsake God's Word so that they might have control and pre-eminence. Like Amaziah tried to intimidate Amos, I have been in churches where the most outspoken people have their way, whether or not it is biblical, because others were intimidated by them. Encountering opposition is a part of ministry. Motyer keenly observes,

> There is no service of God without opposition, persecution and trial. This truth lies on the surface of the story before us, and it is well worth our while to face it and accept that it is so. How often servants of God are knocked off course by the onset of difficulties and oppositions! The Scripture is surely plain enough that we are not to *be surprised at the fiery ordeal which comes upon you to prove*

---

12. Hans Christian Andersen, *The Emperor's New Clothes*, trans. Jean Hersholt [online]; accessed 1 December 2009; available from http://www.andersen.sdu.dk/vaerk/hersholt/TheEmperorsNewClothes_e.html; Internet.

you (1 Pet. 4:12), yet that is often exactly what we are—surprised! Amos met his tests and oppositions and so shall we.[13]

Amos experienced such opposition; Jesus and the apostles experienced such opposition; so why should the Lord's servants expect any less today? Moreover, like Amos, Jesus, and the apostles, we must stand firm in the face of resistance.

Is it the prophet?

Amos' response reveals his reason for coming to Israel and the basis of the authority of his message.[14] First, he had never been a professional prophet. Many prophets made a living prophesying, but Amos was not one of them. Second, Amos never received formal training as a prophet. His background was purely secular. Third, he had no financial need to become a prophet. Before coming to preach, he was involved in breeding or the marketing end of animal husbandry, which may have been with cattle, sheep, or goats. Also, Amos said he was a grower of sycamore trees. They were highly valued in antiquity. The sycamore fruit was grown in abundance as a food source even though it was smaller and inferior in quality to the common fig. Just before the sycamore figs ripened someone needed to split them open with a special knife in order to ensure proper ripening in the following days.[15] The wood of the sycamore tree was a valued source of soft lumber, which was used extensively in Egypt for utensils and mummy cases.[16] Both of Amos' occupations would have been common in Israel and Judah's society. Many made their livelihoods doing the same work Amos had been doing. Most people were either shepherds or farmers.

---

13. Motyer, 170.
14. Hubbard discusses the interplay of 'seer' and 'prophet' suggesting in Israel those who preached concerning matters of morality were called 'prophets,' and in Judah they were called 'seers.' For this reason, (1) Amaziah called Amos a seer without Amos' objection, (2) the mention of 'seer' is followed by a command to return to Judah and prophesy, (3) Amos acknowledges he is not a 'prophet' and that his authority to preach in the north comes directly from the Lord's command, and (4) Amos seems to renounce any concern for prophetic office or any income that might come from it (214).
15. King, 117.
16. R. K. Harrison, 'Sycamore; Sycamore Tree,' in *The International Standard Bible Encyclopedia*, ed. Geoffrey Bromiley, rev. ed. [*ISBE*] (Grand Rapids: Eerdmans, 1988), 4:674.

Therefore, Amos' trek north had nothing to do with financial gain. Those in the Lord's service must beware of the temptation to become consumed with money and with worry about how God will provide it. It is easy to move from wondering how God will provide to being consumed with 'making sure' God will provide. Living in a society consumed with materialism like Israel was in Amos' day and like the society most of us live in today, it is a great temptation. We must do as Jesus said and seek first His kingdom and righteousness, trusting Him to provide what we need (Matt. 6:33).

The reason Amos gave for being in Israel was because 'the LORD took me from following the flock, and the LORD said to me, "Go, prophesy to my people Israel"' (7:15). The prophet did not prophesy under his own authority. Those of us who preach God's Word must not forget that we have no authority in ourselves. Amos had the authority of vocation, God's call upon his life; he had the authority of revelation, God's Word; and he had the authority of commission when God told him to 'go.'[17] Likewise, our authority is in God's call upon our lives (vocation), in His inerrant Word (revelation), and in His declaration to go into the entire world and make disciples (commission).

It is the Lord!

The ultimate authority in Israel, and indeed in all of creation, is the Lord. Governments and their leaders may be impressed with themselves, but they come and go. Institutionalized religion may become influential, but it is temporary. Servants of the Lord may speak to thousands, but they have no authority of their own. Every authority rises and falls under the ultimate authority of the Lord Jesus Christ (Matt. 28:18). It is Christ and His Church that will stand.

Under the Lord's authority, Amos responded to Amaziah. Amaziah may have told Amos to stop preaching, but Amos listened to the Lord and was not intimidated by Amaziah. One will find courage when one submits to God's authority and will for one's life. Amos' declaration of God's Word was in contrast to Amaziah's word. His message was fivefold. First, Amaziah's

---

17. Motyer, 172.

wife would become a prostitute in order to live. Amos was not a prophet who was a 'spiritual prostitute' selling his craft for financial gain, but Amaziah's wife would have to sell herself just to survive. Second, all of Amaziah's children will be killed, ending his line. Amaziah chided Amos for foretelling the end of the house of Jeroboam. Now, he will suffer the same fate. Third, Amaziah will lose his land. His inheritance and heritage would be no more. Fourth, he will be sent into exile in an unclean land. This punishment is especially severe to a priest. In an unclean land he could no longer perform his duties as a priest because he would be unclean himself. The one who tried to prohibit Amos from his calling would no longer be able to fulfill what he claimed to be his calling.[18] Fifth, Amos quoted Amaziah and declared Israel certainly would go into exile (7:11). The priest of Bethel will witness first-hand what he so strongly opposed in Amos' message.

One treads on dangerous ground when one opposes the messenger of the Lord. The Bible records several occasions when individuals failed to respect God's servant and opposed him to their detriment. Notice a few examples. Korah led a rebellion against Moses, and the earth opened up and devoured Korah and all those who were with him (Num. 16:1-40). Children from Bethel mocked God's prophet, Elisha, and forty-two of them were torn to pieces by bears (2 Kings 2:23-24). A captain of Israel declared what Elisha prophesied would not happen and was trampled to death (2 Kings 7:1-20). The false prophet, Hananiah, opposed Jeremiah and died as a result (Jer. 28:1-17). Why were the results of their opposition to God's servants so terrible? It is because their opposition was not just against the authority of the messenger but against the authority of the Lord God. It was under God's authority these prophets preached, so it was against God's authority these people rebelled.

Reminders
When it comes to authority, Amos reminds us that we must obey God rather than man. There is ultimately only one authority to whom we answer, and that is the Lord. Amos also reminds preachers that whenever they faithfully proclaim

---

18. W. Rudolph, *Joel-Amos-Obadiah-Jonah*, Kommentar zum Alten Testament 23/2, ed. E. Sellin (Gütersloh: Gerd Mohn, 1971), 259.

God's Word, they can expect opposition. Many times that opposition comes from religious leaders, the very people they would hope would stand beside them and support them. The apostles experienced such opposition before the religious council and the high priest, who said, 'We strictly charged you not to teach in this name, yet here you have filled Jerusalem with your teaching, and you intend to bring this man's blood upon us.' But Peter and the apostles answered, 'We must obey God rather than men' (Acts 5:28-29). Amos reminds preachers that their authority in serving the Lord comes from God's call upon their lives and His Word. Ultimately, they live before and preach before an audience of one. And Amos reminds any of us of the severe consequences of trying to usurp God's authority.

Study Questions

1. What were the causes of Amos' opposition?
2. Why should God's people not be surprised by governmental opposition to God's people and message?
3. How do people use religion to oppose the things of God?
4. What causes some religious people to become resistant to God's Word?
5. Why is opposition from religious leaders so difficult to understand?
6. How did Amos respond to his opposition?
7. Why is the issue of authority significant to God's messenger?

12

The End of a Season
(Amos 8:1-14)

College basketball reigns in the American states of Indiana and Kentucky. I had heard it to be the case, but I have witnessed it first-hand since I moved to southern Indiana, just across the Ohio River from Louisville, Kentucky. Becoming a pastor of a church in Indiana and attending seminary in Kentucky made me realize that I needed to educate myself in college basketball if I were to understand and relate to the people in the area. I realized college basketball was taken seriously when a deacon's wife in the church where I was pastor reworded a Bible verse and said, 'As the Father has sent me, so send IU (Indiana University).' She was joking, but she made her point concerning the importance of IU basketball. I have been amazed at the media coverage of college basketball. As the season approaches and continues to its climax of March Madness, college basketball sometimes dominates the news. I have often thought that if a meteorite were to strike Jefferson County at the time the University of Louisville Cardinals were playing the University of Kentucky Wildcats, it might make the headlines if it landed on the Louisville's coliseum or somehow affected travel to the game. Otherwise, it would maybe make page ten.

As the season approaches, great anticipation swells as people speculate on how well their teams will perform, and as soon as the season ends, fans are already talking about their prospects for next year. With all of the hype before and after the season, one thing is true. Every season has a beginning and an end. Each season begins with a first game, and each ends with the championship game of the Final Four. At that point, the record books are closed. The season is over. In Amos 8, Amos receives a vision and then delivers a message where the Lord indicates Israel's season of existence will quickly come to an end. It too had a beginning when the Lord formed Israel and established His covenant with the nation. Then again, like every other season, it too will have an end as the Lord brings His judgment upon His people, Israel.

Look at the coming judgment (8:1-3)
The passage begins with Amos receiving a vision from the Lord. In this vision, Amos sees a basket of summer fruit. Many say that the significance of this vision is to let Amos see that Israel is 'ripe for judgment.'[1] Certainly, Israel is ripe for judgment, but the greater significance is in what type of fruit Amos sees, 'summer fruit.' Otherwise, any ripe fruit in a basket would suffice to communicate the idea of 'ripe for judgment.' Therefore, it is beneficial to have some knowledge of Israel's agricultural calendar in order to appreciate the significance of 'summer fruit' in the vision.

In his excavations of Gezer in 1908, R. A. S. Macalister uncovered what is now called the Gezer Calendar.[2] It dates to about 925 B.C., not many years after the death of Solomon, and lays out the sequence of ancient Israel's agricultural year. The inscription is as follows:

> Months of vintage and olive harvest;
> months of sowing;
> months of spring pasture;
> months of flax pulling;
> month of barley harvest;
> month of wheat harvest and measuring;
> months of pruning;
> month of summer fruit. *Margin*: Abijah[3]

---

1. Finley, 260.
2. H. W. Perkins, 'Gezer Calendar,' in *The International Standard Bible Encyclopedia*, ed. Geoffrey W. Bromiley, rev. ed. [*ISBE*] (Grand Rapids: Eerdmans, 1982), 2:460.
3. Bill T. Arnold and Bryan E. Beyer, *Readings from the Ancient Near East* (Grand Rapids: Baker Academic, 2002), 171.

Amos 8:1-14

The inscription begins with a two month period of olive harvest that goes from mid-September to mid-November. Next comes a two-month period of planting wheat and barley from mid-November to mid-January. This period is followed by a period of planting chickpeas, melons, and cucumbers from the end of January to March. The end of March through the end of April consisted of hoeing flax used to make cords and linen cloth. The month from April to May was the barley harvest. Next was a month of wheat harvest in May to June, and then came two months of grape harvest in all of June and July. The last month of Israel's agricultural year was August, producing the summer fruit, which consisted of figs, grapes, pomegranates, and other fruits.[4]

The summer fruit was the last to come in Israel's agricultural calendar. It came at the end of the season. Therefore, just as Israel's agricultural cycle had an end, so will Israel as a nation. The fruit Israel produced was a lack of compassion for those in need, a lack of justice for those who could not defend themselves, and a lack of sincere worship before the Lord. It will be the last fruit the northern kingdom will ever produce. Having been one who had harvested figs of the summer fruit and one who was communicating to an agrarian society, Amos and his audience surely had no difficulty understanding the Lord's message in this vision.

Nevertheless, Amos the preacher further emphasized his message with a play on words. In Hebrew, the word 'summer fruit' is *qayic* and the word 'end' is *qēc*. Inscriptional evidence from Samaria from the time of Amos and Hosea suggests the people in the northern kingdom had a dialect such that they shortened the vowel combination in words like *qayic*, so that when they pronounced the word *qayic*, it sounded like *qēc*. In other words, this prophet from the south pronounced the Hebrew words for 'summer fruit' and 'end' so that they sounded exactly the same, the way people in the north pronounced them.[5] His word play was an observable way of communicating that the summer fruit, which came at the

---

4. Howard F. Vos, *Nelson's New Illustrated Bible Manners & Customs* (Nashville: Thomas Nelson Publishers, 1999), 140.
5. Finley, 262; John C. L. Gibson, *Textbook of Syrian Semitic Inscriptions*, 2 vols. (Oxford: Clarendon, 1971), 1:7-8.

end of Israel's agricultural cycle, represented the end of the northern kingdom in his vision.

Furthermore, the Lord will no longer pass by Israel. In Egypt, God instructed the Israelites to put the blood of lambs on the doorposts so that when the angel of death came, he would pass by (Exod. 12:22-23). Because of the blood, the people experienced salvation from God's judgment, but now the Lord says He will no longer pass by Israel. Israel will no longer be safe from God's judgment. Once again, there will be blood, but it will be the blood of the people of Israel. The carnage will be such that there will be bodies everywhere. In their temple, where once the joyous singing was the only noise to the Lord, there will be the din of wailing and howling. Their temple will be filled with 'an inarticulate, shattering scream such as is found in primitive funerary laments and in the face of sudden catastrophe.'[6] Then, there will be a call for silence. How can they rightly mourn when they have received what they rightly deserved?[7] They may think the Lord will come back and continue with the devastation. Maybe they will be so overwhelmed that there will be no words to say. Maybe they will cry until there simply will be no more tears. What a reversal! Motyer rightly observes:

> This then is the situation. Their religion had utterly failed to alert them to a God of judgment and therefore the fact would spring upon them all unready, when their expectations were all geared to diametrically opposite outcomes.[8]

Like Amos, we live in a society that rejects and scoffs at such messages. And like Amos, we desperately need believers with the courage to proclaim God's impending judgment on those who reject God's Word. It may be that if there were mourning over sin now, there would not be mourning as a result of God's judgment later. It is then the weeping may end and turn into glorious praise as God's people worship the Lord who has shown them mercy and grace through faith in Jesus Christ. Messages aimed with the sole purpose of making people feel good about themselves will ultimately result in disaster.

---

6. A. Baumann, 'יָלַל yll,' in *Theological Dictionary of the Old Testament*, ed. G. J. Botterweck and H. Ringgren [*TDOT*] (Grand Rapids: Eerdmans, 1990), 6:82.
7. See Ezekiel 24:16-24.
8. Motyer, 178.

Messages with the sole aim of exalting Christ crucified for the sins of the world will result in salvation for those who believe.

Listen to the reasons for the coming judgment (8:4-6)
God wanted to make sure Israel fully comprehended His message. Therefore, it is interesting to note how the Lord communicated with Israel. He used various means to convey His message. First, the Lord showed a vision to Amos to present a picture of what will happen, so that Amos could describe it to the people (vv. 1-3). Second, the Lord declared the reasons for the coming events. Third, the Lord God employed the repetition of motifs He had used earlier in Amos' message as He addressed the reasons for the coming judgment. Repetition is the mother of all learning. The variety of rhetorical methods reveals that God gave the people every opportunity to understand the message and repent. When what Amos describes and proclaims does come to pass, the people will not be able to say they were unable to understand the warning God had given them through His prophet.

(1) Their greed outweighed any concern for the needy (8:4)
The first reason Amos gives for the coming judgment is that the greed of the wealthy had eliminated any compassion they might have had for those in need. One might wonder how people became poor and needy in Israel since every family had an inheritance of land that was given them from the Lord.[9] One way was through what might be called natural causes such as the death of one's parents or of a husband as was the case with Naomi and Ruth. In a male-dominated society, the husband was the main provider for the family. His death would have severe consequences for widows without sons to care for them. The hardship was that much more difficult for orphans. Therefore, laws concerning widows and orphans existed because of this reality. For example, the law states,

> You shall not mistreat any widow or fatherless child. If you do mistreat them, and they cry out to me, I will surely hear their cry, and my wrath will burn, and I will kill you with the sword, and

---

9. See Christopher J. H. Wright, *Old Testament Ethics for the People of God* (Downer Grove, IL: InterVarsity Press, 2004), 169-70.

your wives shall become widows and your children fatherless (Exod. 22:22-24).

You shall not pervert the justice due to the sojourner or to the fatherless, or take a widow's garment in pledge, but you shall remember that you were a slave in Egypt and the Lord your God redeemed you from there; therefore I command you to do this. When you reap your harvest in your field and forget a sheaf in the field, you shall not go back to get it. It shall be for the sojourner, the fatherless, and the widow, that the Lord your God may bless you in all the work of your hands. When you beat your olive trees, you shall not go over them again. It shall be for the sojourner, the fatherless, and the widow. When you gather the grapes of your vineyard, you shall not strip it afterward. It shall be for the sojourner, the fatherless, and the widow. You shall remember that you were a slave in the land of Egypt; therefore I command you to do this (Deut. 24:17-22).

The book of Proverbs teaches another possible way someone may have become impoverished was because of one's own laziness and the squandering of one's resources. While hard work did not ensure economic prosperity, in general it certainly was conducive to it.[10] However, the Old Testament recognizes oppression as the greatest cause of poverty. Most people become poor as the result of the actions of others. So much attention in Scripture is given to this cause that Leslie J. Hoppe concludes:

> The prophets ... did not regard poverty as the result of chance, destiny or laziness. Poverty was simply the creation of the rich who have broken the covenant because of their greed. The wealthy used their abilities and resources not to enhance the community but to support their own purpose. In this way they violated the covenant, they destroyed the unity of Israel and called forth divine judgment.[11]

Amos describes an extremely callous and harsh environment where the wealthy 'trampled' on the needy and literally caused the needy 'to cease' or to be 'annihilated.' A society that was founded on covenantal impartiality and communal support became a society of brutality and exploitation.

---

10. Proverbs 12:11; 14:23; 20:13; 21:17.
11. Leslie J. Hoppe, *Being Poor: A Biblical Study* (Wilmington, DE: Michael Glazier, 1987), 61.

The law had much to say concerning Israel's responsibility to care for the poor.[12] First, according to Leviticus 25, the people were responsible to care for the poor regardless of the cause of their impoverishment.[13] Certainly, the spiritual leaders needed to deal with the cause, but it was not the place of the people to determine who they would or would not help if there was a need. Second, families were to play an important role in preventing poverty and restoring those burdened with it from within the family.[14] Third, taken in its entirety the law provided a type of welfare system for those without land or male providers.[15] Fourth, the law emphasized the responsibility of those who are wealthy and powerful when it comes to poverty instead of lecturing or blaming the poor concerning their impoverished condition. Therefore,

> Israel's law puts the focus instead on those who actually have the power to do something, or whose power must be constrained in some way for the benefit of the poor. Thus the law addresses the creditor, not the debtor (Deut. 24:6, 10-13); employers, not day laborers (Deut. 24:14); slave-owners, not slaves (Exod. 21:20-21, 26-27; Deut. 15:12-18).[16]

Fifth, the law indicated Israel's motivation for showing compassion to the needy should have been because the Lord had shown compassion on Israel. Their kindness to the poor imitated the Lord and demonstrated Israel's gratitude to God (Deut. 24:22). Sixth, obedience in caring for the poor was an indication of obedience to the rest of the law and God's covenant with Israel. Moses told the Israelites:

> When you have finished paying all the tithe of your produce in the third year, which is the year of tithing, giving it to the Levite, the sojourner, the fatherless, and the widow, so that they may eat within your towns and be filled, then you shall say before the LORD your God, 'I have removed the sacred portion out of my house, and moreover, I have given it to the Levite, the sojourner, the fatherless, and the widow, according to all your commandment that you have commanded me. I have not

---

12. See Wright's detailed discussion, *Old Testament Ethics*, 172-5.
13. Leviticus 25:25, 35, 39, 47.
14. Leviticus 25:23; Numbers 26:52-56; Deuteronomy 25:5-10.
15. Exodus 23:10-11; Deuteronomy 14:28-29; 15:1-18; 24:18-22.
16. Wright, *Old Testament Ethics*, 174.

transgressed any of your commandments, nor have I forgotten them' (Deut. 26:12-13).

C. J. H. Wright comments:

> Thus, giving to the needy is not only a sacred duty to God, but it also is the defining point for any claim to have kept the law. *The law is kept only if the poor are cared for.* Only when Israel responds to the needy by enabling *everyone* in the community to eat and be satisfied can they affirm I have done *everything* that you commanded me. This shows ... how the enacted love for the poor and needy is the practical proof of genuine, God-honoring love for the neighbor. The Torah itself thus agrees with the way the prophets later pinpoint and prioritize care for the poor as somehow definitive or paradigmatic of Israel's response to God as a whole.[17]

The violent abuse of the poor in Amos' day exposed not only the disdain of the wealthy and powerful toward the needy in their society, but also it exposed their utter contempt toward God.

(2) Their greed outweighed any commitment to God (8:5)
According to the book of Amos, the people of Israel were obviously very religious. Verse 5 provides another example of their religious practices. The new moon festival appears to have been prominent even though the Old Testament gives it little attention in comparison to other festivals. Other passages imply the people ceased all work at this time, but this verse is the only one to mention it explicitly.[18] The merchants were faithful to attend these gatherings set aside for celebration and worshiping the Lord, but their hearts were not in it. While the various activities of the service were happening, these businessmen were planning out their next business transaction, and their anticipation of making a profit was more important than their worshiping the Lord. To others, their facade of religiosity may have covered up their selfish greed, but the Lord knew what was in their hearts.

Apparently, their times of worship were necessary inconveniences, necessary for their reputations and necessary to

---

17. Christopher J. H. Wright, *Deuteronomy*, New International Biblical Commentary, Old Testament Series (Peabody: Hendrickson; Carlisle: Paternoster, 1996), 271-2.

18. Paul, 257-58; see 1 Samuel 20:5; 2 Kings 4:23; Isaiah 1:13-14; Ezekiel 46:1, 3; Hosea 2:13.

receive God's blessings. It reminds me of what I have witnessed in a number of Christian schools. At all levels of education, many require attendance for chapel services. On numerous occasions I have seen both teachers and students working on some assignment during a chapel service. Certainly, they were fulfilling their obligation to attend, but it is difficult to believe they were truly focused on worshiping the Lord. It appeared the chapel service was a necessary inconvenience for them.

A person might think the problem Amos confronted merely was that the people were thinking about making money more than worshiping the Lord, but the problem he confronted was far deeper. The problem was that they were focused on themselves more than they were focused on worshiping the Lord. They were self-serving in their thoughts and actions. Put this way, how much of our thinking in times of worship is self-serving rather than God-honoring? How much of our attendance at worship meetings is unaccompanied by a deep desire to worship the Lord with God's people? How much of it is out of obligation so that we may say we did what God and others expected us to do? How much of the time is spent thinking about what we will do when the service is over? It seems that those most susceptible to such thoughts are those who have attended so many worship services they have become commonplace. Attending worship services can become merely part of a routine. It is like when we brush our teeth every morning; as we brush many of us often think about what we are going to be doing the rest of the day rather than concentrating on brushing our teeth the way the dentist has instructed us. We have heard it is good for us, and we believe we need to do it. However, we give it little thought as we do. Thinking about other things when one puts on the facade of worshiping the Lord is as appalling as a husband thinking about other things when he is supposedly being intimate with his wife.

(3) Their greed outweighed any conviction relating to integrity (8:5)
The Sabbath was another day the people were supposed to abstain from labor (Exod. 20:8-10). As with the new moon festival, the businessmen of Israel observed the Sabbath, but they resented having to do so. What's more, Amos revealed what they were doing when they were conducting business. They were

literally 'making small the ephah', their standard unit of measure for grain. The ephah, meaning 'basket', was the basic unit for dry measure. It represents about 22 litres in today's standards. Also, they were 'making great the shekel,' their standard unit weight. The shekel would weigh about 11.5 grams today.[19] In other words, they were shorting people on the amount they received by using smaller baskets and tampering with the weights and scales. Thus, the merchants were 'making the shekel great' in their pockets too. What's more, they apparently mixed the refuse of the wheat, the chaff, in with the grain (8:6). It added to the weight of the sell, but it was worthless and inhumane.

The law clearly indicated that justice should dictate all matters in Israel, especially when it came to the people's business affairs. People were to conduct themselves with integrity as they engaged in commerce. For this reason, the Lord God states in His law: 'You shall do no wrong in judgment, in measures of length or weight or quantity. You shall have just balances, just weights, a just ephah, and a just hin: I am the LORD your God, who brought you out of the land of Egypt' (Lev. 19:35-36). Such laws were prevalent in the pagan nations of the ancient Near East too.[20] As we are reminded in the world today, no society can stand when dishonesty goes unchecked, yet we are plagued with it in every sphere of society. Furthermore, the Lord clearly communicated His feelings concerning those who practice such dishonesty:

> You shall not have in your bag two kinds of weights, a large and a small. You shall not have in your house two kinds of measures, a large and a small. A full and fair weight you shall have, a full and fair measure you shall have, that your days may be long in the land that the LORD your God is giving you. For all who do such things, all who act dishonestly, are an abomination to the LORD your God (Deut. 25:13-16).[21]

The wealthy in Israel hypocritically acted as if keeping the law was their deepest conviction, but in truth, they valued profit over all else. As a result, Israel's use of dishonest measures is

---

19. M. Pierce Matheney, 'Weights and Measures,' in *Holman Illustrated Bible Dictionary*, ed. Chad Brand, Charles Draper, Archie England (Nashville: Holman Bible Publishers, 2003), 1665-8.
20. Paul, 259.
21. Wright, *Old Testament Ethics*, 166-7.

one of the reasons for God's judgment; it is one of the reasons Israel's days will not be 'long in the land.'

(4) Their greed outweighed any consideration for people (8:6)
As if all that Amos mentioned was not enough already, showing how Israel deserved God's judgment, he continued pointing out how the wealthy not only traded in grain but in human trafficking. In 2:6, Amos revealed they were selling the poor into debt slavery. Here, he condemns their buying these slaves for themselves. According to the law, the Israelites were forbidden to enslave other Israelites (Lev. 25:42-43, 46, 53, 55). They were supposed to treat those Israelite brothers in their service as hired hands paying off debts. The law even protected foreigners who were slaves. The people of Israel should not have forgotten they too were slaves at one time, and the Lord redeemed their freedom and treated them with kindness. Nevertheless, the wealthy in Amos' day valued profit over people, and to them it was all the better if they could profit by buying, selling, and using people.

Israel was no different from the neighboring pagan nations that engaged in human trafficking (1:6, 9). They were no different from those who had abused them in Egypt. Therefore, they were just as guilty and deserving of judgment as the pagan nations around them. Moreover, by acting like the other nations, Israel lost its distinctiveness as God's people. Instead of pointing the nations to the Lord, Israel became a reproach to God before the nations. Israel compromised its mission and purpose by becoming like the other nations. Has materialism so taken us that we have become self-serving in our motives and actions too? Does our greed outweigh our concern for the needy, our commitment to God, our conviction relating to integrity, or our consideration for people? How much has the Church compromised God's mission and purpose by being so much like the world that unbelievers see no distinction in us?

Learn of your future (8:7-10)
As elsewhere in Amos' message, after revealing what the people of Israel have done he told his audience what the Lord will do. First, the Lord vowed He will not forget the wealthy's greed and their disregard for Him and others. It is

the third time Amos indicated the Lord made a solemn oath. First He swore by His holiness (4:2), and then He swore by Himself (6:8). In this instance, He swore by the 'the pride of Jacob.' This term may be a little confusing since the Lord previously said He abhorred the pride of Jacob (6:8). One possibility is that God was ironically swearing upon that which had condemned Israel, her pride in her military and economic strength.[22] Another way of understanding it may be by recognizing the distinction between what had become the pride of Jacob (its strongholds and all the possessions they protect) and who was supposed to be the pride of Jacob (the Lord God). The Lord would only swear upon that which was lasting and trustworthy. How could he swear upon Samaria and its strongholds when they were going to be destroyed unless He was referring to Israel's eternal inheritance?[23] While that too is a possibility, given the other two times the Lord swore upon Himself, it is more likely here again that the Lord swore by Himself.[24] He was the only one who was eternal and trustworthy, and He was the only true pride of Jacob whether or not the people acknowledged this truth.

Second, the rhetorical question of verse 8 anticipated the Lord's anger as Amos described it being like an earthquake and the flooding of the Nile River. Earthquakes have always been common in this region. It is because the Jordan Rift Valley is part of the Afro-Arabian Rift Valley, the longest, deepest, and widest fissure in the earth's surface. It extends as far north as southeastern Turkey and as far south as Ethiopia, where it splits. Also, from this primary rift several secondary fractures spread out that 'virtually make a geologic mosaic of Israel'. According to seismographic registrations, between 200 and 300 tremors occur in Israel every day. Most are undetectable by humans, but on several occasions throughout history earthquakes have caused a great amount of destruction and have been responsible for thousands of deaths in Israel.[25]

---

22. Hubbard, 221; Paul, 260.
23. Niehaus, 472.
24. Finley, 302-3; Garrett, 243-4; Billy K. Smith, 147.
25. Barry J. Beitzel, *The Moody Atlas of Bible Lands* (Chicago: Moody Press, 1985), 37-8.

Amos' introduction attests to the impact of an earthquake upon the region (1:1).

Therefore, it should not be surprising that several biblical writers compared God's wrath to a trembling of the earth. For instance, Isaiah described the Lord's judgment in this way:

The earth is utterly broken, the earth is split apart, the earth is violently shaken. The earth staggers like a drunken man; it sways like a hut; its transgression lies heavy upon it, and it falls, and will not rise again (Isa. 24:19-20).[26]

The idea of a destructive earthquake must have been terrifying to Israel. Amos said God's judgment will be likened to a devastating earthquake resulting in the mourning of all of Israel.

Another phenomenon well known in that part of the world was the annual flooding of the Nile River that began in June and did not completely recede until around October. The farmers planted their seeds in the muddy soil during October or November and harvested their crops from January to March.[27] There were times the Nile's flooding was very destructive. Just as the flooding of the Nile lasted for several months, the analogy may point to Israel's cataclysm lasting for an extended period of time.[28] Israel will be lifted up, shaken, and then brought down. Like the swift-moving destructive swell of a churning river that has surged over its banks, Israel's judgment will come swiftly, with lasting and detrimental results.

Not only will the earth be affected by God's judgment but the heavens too. Both the heavens and the earth will lay bare God's wrath. Here God declared that at the brightest time of day there will be a total eclipse of the sun.[29] Amos had already declared the Day of the Lord will be a day of darkness and not light (5:18, 20). Many people in the ancient Near East considered eclipses as evil omens indicating the wrath of the gods.[30] The sky will proclaim God's fury as He deals with Israel.

---

26. See Psalm 77:18; Proverbs 30:21; Joel 2:10; Habakkuk 3:6; Zechariah 14:4.
27. Carl G. Rasmussen, *Zondervan NIV Atlas of the Bible* (Grand Rapids: Zondervan Publishing House, 1989), 57.
28. Billy K. Smith, 148.
29. See Joel 2:10 for another example of an earthquake and eclipse describing God's judgment.
30. Paul, 263.

The mourning of the people of Israel will be the outcome. Their celebratory songs of joy will turn into mournful laments of grief. Instead of wearing flamboyant attire to make a display of offering their 'best' to the Lord as they attended their religious feasts, they will put on the clothes of bitter sadness and shave their heads as an indication of their great sorrow. They will be overcome with bereavement such as that which overtakes parents who have lost an only child, one of the most severe of all calamities.[31] It will truly be a bitter day.

Latch on to God's Word before it is too late (8:11-14)
It is easy to fail to recognize the value of people and things until we lose them. Only after the loss do we often begin to appreciate the impact they had on our lives. Such was the case with Israel when it came to God's Word. Of all of the nations in the entire earth, Israel was the only one to have received the inspired written Word of God. By the time of Amos, several generations of Israel had the privilege of hearing God's Word since the beginning of the nation. Furthermore, the people of Israel had the blessing of the prophets of God proclaiming God's Word to them in their present. It was a fresh Word from the Lord directly meant for them to hear. One would think they would have been eager to listen to whatever God's messenger said and quick to obey it, but this response was not the case.

Instead, the people had become so used to seeing and hearing God's Word that they failed to really take notice and listen to the message. They became like Israel as described by Isaiah: 'He sees many things, but does not observe them; his ears are open, but he does not hear' (Isa. 42:20). Therefore, the Lord declared He would send a famine. This famine will be different from the others of which Amos spoke. It will be a famine of God's Word. Many, like Amaziah, will get what they wanted, namely, the prophets to cease prophesying.

One may make some observations concerning God's Word from this text. First, true life comes from God's Word. The Lord says the people will stagger everywhere looking for God's Word like one who is desperately hungry and thirsty but to no avail.

---

31. See Jeremiah 6:26; Zechariah 12:10.

Amos 8:1-14

They will fall never to rise again. One of the last statements Moses said to Israel was, 'Take to heart all the words by which I am warning you today, that you may command them to your children, that they may be careful to do all the words of this law. For it is no empty word for you, but your very life, and by this word you shall live long in the land that you are going over the Jordan to possess' (Deut. 32:46-47). It was God's Word that was Israel's life, and it was only God's Word that could revive them (Ps. 19:7). Apart from God's Word the nation could not survive, thus the famine of God's Word will make God's judgment upon Israel complete. The people either forgot or took too lightly the magnitude of God's Word upon their lives.

How many people in the Church today either forget or take too lightly the magnitude of God's Word upon their lives? There is no substitute for God's Word. As the Creator, the Lord reveals that He exists and puts on display His divine attributes, but it is the written Word of God that tells us that the way to a restored relationship with the Creator is by faith in His Son, the Lord Jesus Christ. It is the written Word of God that establishes Jesus is the Messiah, the Son of God, and the Word of Life. It is the written Word of God that reveals God's ways to His children and His will for them. That being said, why do so many in the Church diminish the centrality of the Word of God? It happens when leaders fail to study God's Word. It happens when so much time is given to other things, sometimes worthwhile things, in corporate worship that inadequate time is given to the reading of and proclamation of God's Word. It happens when churches fail to properly disciple their people in God's Word. It happens when believers neglect reading and meditating on God's Word throughout the week.

However, what truly is appalling is when leaders do provide the people with ample opportunities and encouragement to learn and apply God's Word only for people to spend years in the church and believe that since they are reading it and hearing it they must then have it in their hearts and minds. It is like a student in a calculus class who has a knowledgeable teacher on the subject. The student may follow every step the teacher shows the class. Walking out of the class the student may feel confident about the material. However, if the student cannot do the homework later on, then the student has learned only one thing—the teacher knows calculus. It is only when the student can do the problems (and I might add communicate the information to someone else) that the student has learned the material. Like this student, there are many who have listened to sermons and sat in Bible studies for years thinking that since they have attended these studies they have learned everything they have heard, but it is only with prayer, meditation, and concentrated effort that one will really learn God's Word so as to apply it. My professor used to say, 'Calculus is not a spectator sport.' Neither is learning and applying God's Word.

Second, a person's opportunity to rightly respond to God's Word will not last forever. The Lord says that in the day when judgment has come the people will hunger and thirst for God's Word, but they will not find it. It will be too late. The privilege of hearing God's Word is not eternal for those who reject it. There may be a time when people's hearts become so hardened they will not be able to respond to God's Word when they hear it (Heb. 3:7-13). Others will die without rightly responding to God's Word. God's Word comes with a sense of urgency. The Lord says the young people will faint. Therefore, even young people should beware. A hardened heart or a last breath may come sooner than one thinks. Those with the brightest futures will have no future without the life-giving Word of God. What's more, without its youth, what hope can a nation have in its future?

Third, substitutes for God's Word leave people wanting. As already noted, Jeroboam I established a new cult so that the people in Israel would go to these shrines instead of to Jerusalem in Judah. Therefore, he established two national shrines, one at Bethel in the south and the other at Dan in the north, as substitutes. Amos' term, 'The Guilt of Samaria' probably is a pejorative term for the cultic site at Bethel. Amos' contemporary, Hosea, referred to it as 'The Calf of Samaria' (Hosea 8:6) and 'The Sin of Israel' (Hosea 10:8).[32] The second place Amos mentioned was Dan in reference to its god. Thirdly, Amos again referred to the people's pilgrimages to Beersheba (5:5). Amos' reference to these three places appears to be a way

---

32. Paul, 270-1.

of encapsulating the sum of Israel's false religion as a twisted understanding of the Lord God.[33] Israel's commitment was to *their* established religious practices rather than to God and His Word as He had revealed Himself to Israel. Their religious cult was supposedly established in the Lord's name, but it was not according to His Word. It was much like Jesus described people when He quoted Isaiah saying, 'This people honors me with their lips, but their heart is far from me; in vain do they worship me, teaching as doctrines the commandments of men' (Mark 7:6-7). As a result of their disregard for God's Word in Amos' day, the end is fast approaching. The people will thirst for God's Word, yet they will be disappointed. The people and their false religion will fall never to rise again. Israel's season is coming to an end.

STUDY QUESTIONS

1. What is the meaning of the ripe basket of 'summer fruit' Amos saw in his vision?

2. What had been the 'fruit' of Israel?

3. What is meant by the Lord will no longer 'pass by' Israel? What does this idea reveal about God?

4. Are there any similarities between Israel's response to Amos's message of judgment and people's response to a message of God's judgment today?

5. What is the significance of Amos' way of declaring God's judgment?

6. What did God's law have to say concerning care for the poor?

7. How did Amos' message show the necessity of God's Word?

---

33. Some assert these are references to the worship of other gods—Billy K. Smith, 152; Motyer, 189; Hubbard, 225.

13

The Judgment of God
(Amos 9:1-10)

Amos 9:1-10 is marked by finality. It contains the prophet's final words of judgment concerning Israel; it begins with his fifth and final vision; and it gives great detail of Israel's final hours as a nation. Unlike the previous visions, it contains no dialogue between the Lord and Amos. Instead, it contains only the declaration of the Lord's judgment and a vivid description of how He will execute it upon the people.

The certainty of God's judgment (9:1-4)
When Solomon died and Israel and Judah split into two monarchies, Jeroboam I established his cult in Israel as a replacement for worship at the temple in Jerusalem. Jeroboam inaugurated the cult by going to Bethel to offer sacrifices himself at the altar. In the midst of that ceremony, the Lord sent an unnamed prophet from Judah to rebuke Jeroboam and declare the Lord would raise a descendant of David who would one day come and destroy all of the high places of Samaria and Israel. That descendant of David would be Josiah (1 Kings 12:26–13:6). From the time of the prophecy to the time of its fulfillment was about 300 years. Now, about 150 to 160 years after the time Jeroboam established his cult, the Lord sent another prophet from Judah to go to an altar in Israel, most likely at Bethel, Israel's most prestigious religious shrine, to announce the Lord's judgment on Israel again for

her spiritual apostasy. The people had not repented of their sin, and the Lord had not forgotten His promise concerning His judgment.

With time people might begin to think the Lord has forgotten what He has promised, whether it concerns His deliverance or His judgment. One should be reminded of Peter's words concerning the second coming of Christ:

> This is now the second letter that I am writing to you, beloved. In both of them I am stirring up your sincere mind by way of reminder, that you should remember the predictions of the holy prophets and the commandment of the Lord and Savior through your apostles, knowing this first of all, that scoffers will come in the last days with scoffing, following their own sinful desires. They will say, 'Where is the promise of his coming? For ever since the fathers fell asleep, all things are continuing as they were from the beginning of creation.' For they deliberately overlook this fact, that the heavens existed long ago, and the earth was formed out of water and through water by the word of God, and that by means of these the world that then existed was deluged with water and perished. But by the same word the heavens and earth that now exist are stored up for fire, being kept until the day of judgment and destruction of the ungodly. But do not overlook this one fact, beloved, that with the Lord one day is as a thousand years, and a thousand years as one day. The Lord is not slow to fulfil his promise as some count slowness, but is patient toward you, not wishing that any should perish, but that all should reach repentance (2 Pet. 3:1-9).

The 300 years from the time of the Lord's condemnation of Israel's false religion to the time Josiah came was a period of mercy and grace. During that period the Lord sent several prophets like Amos to His people to warn them of the coming judgment if they failed to repent of their sin and turn back to God. Repeatedly the people dismissed God's messengers and disregarded the opportunities God gave them. Therefore, their dismay will rival the people of Noah's day when the rain began to fall. Because the Lord is a merciful and gracious God, it may appear He is never going to execute His judgment, but we must be assured God will keep His promises. God will always forgive people who truly confess sin, repent, and by faith turn back to Him, but ultimately, God will certainly judge those who reject Him. We must not forget this truth.

Amos 9:1-10

I recall an incident when I was a boy where I was misbehaving in the back seat of the car. My father warned me to stop, but I did not listen to him. Finally, he told me that when we got home he was going to give me a spanking. By the time we got home I had forgotten what my father had said. My older brother was trying to look out for me and get me to go to our bedroom, but I told him to leave me alone. A few minutes later my father came to where I was, reminded me of what had happened and of what he had said, and then gave me a spanking. It was a valuable lesson. Not only did I learn I needed to behave in the back seat, but I learned a greater lesson—my father would keep his word when it came to discipline. Such is the case with our heavenly Father. His promises are true.

(1) God's judgment will be scornful
The vision began with Amos seeing the Lord standing by 'the' altar. The place of this altar is unspecified. Some have suggested this altar is the altar at the temple in Jerusalem, but most likely it is the altar at Bethel, given Amos' northern audience, his recent altercation with Amaziah, the priest of Bethel, in the midst of these five visions, and the prominent position the shrine at Bethel held in Israel.

The altar represented many things in Israel. First, it represented God's forgiveness and atonement with Him. Second, the altar was the place to appease the wrath of God as a payment for sin. As a result, third, the altar represented having peace with God. Fourth, the altar represented having fellowship with God. Fifth, the altar represented a place of commitment to God. Sixth, apparently the altar represented protection. There are a few occasions where people revealed their belief that the altar could afford them sanctuary from having to pay for one's offences. Adonijah tried to make it work for him in 1 Kings 1:50-51, and Joab tried to make it work for him in 1 Kings 2:28-29. Exodus 21:13-14 seems to indicate others held to this notion. However, in each of these passages, the text makes it clear the altar will not provide sanctuary for those trying to escape responsibility for their crimes.[1] Seventh and most of all, the altar represented God's presence with His people. As

---
1. Douglas K. Stuart, *Exodus*, in vol. 2 of *The New American Commentary*, ed. E. Ray Clendenen (Nashville: Broadman & Holman Publishers, 2006), 486-7.

the people offered their sacrifices to the Lord, He was there to receive them as a sweet aroma.

These understandings of the altar are what make God's judgment so scornful. He will be present at the altar, but His presence will bring about very different results from what the people will expect. He will not forgive their sin; His wrath will not be appeased; He will not come in peace; their fellowship with God will be broken; their token displays of commitment will be rejected; and they will not be protected from their enemies. In fact, their presumed Protector will be the one coming to destroy them. The one who was willing to give them life will stand at their altar ready to take their lives.

The place where their sins were supposed to be removed became a place where their sins were multiplied. Their altar, along with their superficial religious displays and demonstrations around it, had all been a sham. Amos warned the people to prepare to meet their God because when they do it will be a dreadful day (4:12). God's retribution will begin at the place of their greatest sacrilege. The words of the apostle Peter are appropriate when he said that 'it is time for judgment to begin at the household of God' (1 Pet. 4:17). I once heard a man in jest say, 'My parents had me in church so much as a child that I learned to sin in church.' With Israel it was no joke. Israel was very religious but had learned to sin at the place of worship. How many of God's people multiply sin at their places of worship today?

(2) God's judgment will be inescapable (9:1-4a)
The Lord commands, 'Strike the capitals until the thresholds shake' (9:1). There is no clear indication whom the Lord will be commanding but, given the language concerning an earthquake in His previous message, it may be God will command an earthquake to strike them (8:7-10). In fact, it may be the earthquake to which Amos refers in Amos 1:1. 'Capitals' were the large, elaborately decorated tops of columns that gave support to ceilings and roofs in palaces and temples. Such destruction of the people's most revered shrine would certainly shake their faith as the capitals holding the columns of their sanctuary in their places come crashing down upon their heads.

No one will escape the death the Lord will wield. Those who will not be killed in the earthquake will perish by the sword. People will attempt to flee, but there will be no place they can run that the Lord will not find them. No one will be beyond His reach. Should they dig down to the subterranean domain of Sheol, even then the Lord will snatch them out. Should they climb up to heaven, still the Lord will bring them down. Should they go to Mount Carmel with its forests and multitude of caves, He will find them. If they go to the depths of the sea, then the Lord will command a serpent to bite them. Finally, if they believe they have cheated death by going into captivity, then their captor will slay them. The Lord is over all the earth and every nation. There is no escape from God's judgment. They might run, but they will not be able to hide.

(3) God's judgment will be purposeful (9:4b)
The final statement of verse 4 reinforces the reversal of God's relationship with Israel. In case there is any question, the Lord wants Israel to know what He has purposed in His heart toward them. Elsewhere in the Scriptures, whenever someone uses the phrase 'to fix one's eyes upon,' it always has a positive meaning for its recipient.[2] Nevertheless, in this instance, when God will fix His eyes upon Israel it will be for Israel's harm.[3] The phrase 'for evil and not for good' might raise some questions. Is God saying He is going to do evil? Here is an instance where the study of Hebrew is of great benefit. The Hebrew word translated 'evil' may mean 'evil, harm, wickedness, perverseness, misery, trouble, [or] disaster.'[4] Whenever this word refers to the Lord's actions, it means harm or calamity He will cause as the result of human wickedness. The parallelism in Isaiah 47:11 provides a good example of how one should understand this word in the context of God's declaration of His judgment. In this verse, Isaiah says, 'But evil shall come upon you, which you will not know how to charm away; disaster shall fall upon you,

---

2. Genesis 44:21; Jeremiah 24:6; 39:12; 40:4.
3. Paul, 279.
4. David W. Baker, 'רעע,' in *New International Dictionary of Old Testament Theology & Exegesis*, ed. Willem A. VanGemeren [*NIDOTTE*] (Grand Rapids: Zondervan, 1997), 3:1154.

for which you will not be able to atone; and ruin shall come upon you suddenly, of which you know nothing.' Here the word 'evil' is in parallel with 'disaster' and 'ruin,' all meant to be synonyms. The Lord's intention will not be to do that which is morally wicked (which by His very nature is an impossibility), but He will purpose to do harm to those who have committed such sin.

The sovereignty of God's judgment (9:5-6)

Given Amos' message of Israel's total annihilation, his audience surely had some doubts concerning the legitimacy of such claims. After all, Israel was at the peak of its military superiority over its neighbors. The people enjoyed an economic prosperity only outdone by the riches of Solomon's day. Their commitment to religion was as zealous as it had ever been. Israel was strong, maybe even invincible in the eyes of some. How could all these terrible things Amos spoke of truly happen? Verses 5 and 6 address this question as if the people actually voiced it to Amos.

People have such questions when they fail to contemplate the all-encompassing power of God and His sovereignty over His creation. The title, 'The Lord Yahweh of Hosts' points to the magnitude of God's pre-eminence. He has the power to carry out all that He says He will do. He merely touches the earth and it begins to tremble and shake. The earth's convulsions are likened to the great rising and churning of the Nile River in Egypt. Only the Lord controls the waters of the seas and the rain. Such phenomena are out of human control, but the Lord is over it all. The Creator who dwells in the heavens and has established the foundation of the earth is the God who has infinite power and authority. He is transcendent over heaven and earth. Therefore, nothing is difficult for the Lord, the one whose covenant Israel had broken. Motyer keenly observes:

> God can speak with certainty that there will be no escape for these people anywhere in His universe, because He is God of the whole. He has absolute mastery over all the earth in its physical substance (5a), its human inhabitants (5b) and its condition at any time (5c); the celestial (6a) and the terrestrial (6b) are equally open to His use, and all the elements, represented here by water and earth (6c), are His to do what He will with.

Amos 9:1-10

This then is what the Lord thinks of pretence; this is how He reacts to it; this is His judgment upon it. The essence of the pretence is the throwing of a cloak of religion over a life motivated towards self. This was the sin of the first Jeroboam and of the last Jeroboam (2 Kings 14:23, 24). God and religion were tools whereby self could be secured and life made secure for self.[5]

The impartiality of God's judgment (9:7-10)
Besides Israel's military superiority, economic prosperity, and fervent religious activity, there was one more reason the people had to doubt Amos' words of judgment upon Israel: Israel was God's chosen people, His treasured possession. They had deceived themselves into believing that since their forefathers experienced God's deliverance from Egypt through the Exodus and had entered into a covenant with the Lord, forevermore their nation would be exempt from the judgments God levied against the other nations. In the end, Israel's holiness and faithfulness to God and His mission for Israel were beside the point. They were a privileged people, a people of special status. The fact their ancestors had made a covenant with the Lord obligated the Lord to bless them no matter what. After all, is that not how a loving God should be?

In verses 7-10, the Lord sets out to correct this deluded thinking. He strongly refutes any notion Israel has any initial claim to God's preference over any of the other nations. Initially, Amos communicated Israel was no better than all the other nations by the fact that Israel will be judged like all the other nations. Now, he tells the people how God is directly involved in the affairs of all nations. Just as the Lord had established Israel as a nation, it is the Lord who has raised every nation on the earth. Therefore, the difference between Israel and the other nations is not nearly as great as they imagined it to be.[6] For instance, Cush (or Ethiopia) was a great distance from Israel and a nation which probably seemed rather remote and insignificant to the people. Yet the Lord had as much to do with the establishment of that nation as he did Israel. Israel was no grander than this remote country of which Israel gave little thought.

---

5. Motyer, 195.
6. Garrett, 271.

What's more, it was the Lord who had established Philistia and Aram, Israel's two long-time enemies, as Israel's neighbors. In a way, each of these two nations experienced their own Exodus as the Philistines fled Caphtor[7] and the Arameans fled Kir[8] to come to Israel's borders. Just as the Lord led Israel out of Egypt, so He led these two nations as well. The uniqueness of Israel's Exodus was diminished and afforded them no special status. Therefore, Israel was not better than their enemies. What's more, even though the Lord delivered the Philistines and Arameans from their respective enemies in Caphtor and Kir, His actions did not deliver them from God's judgment upon them for their sins. God shows no impartiality in His grace and judgment, so why should Israel be any different?

In verse 8, the Lord continued saying His eyes were on 'the sinful kingdom,' echoing verse 4 where God said His eyes were fixed upon His people. Apparently, 'the sinful kingdom' is Israel. His message to the sinful kingdom is clear: the Lord will destroy it. So the Lord says He will destroy the nation of Israel from the face of the earth. However, the following statement appears to contradict what the Lord has just said: 'except that I will not utterly destroy the house of Jacob.' In other words, the sinful northern kingdom of Israel will cease to exist as a nation, but the Lord will preserve for Himself a remnant of the house of Jacob. God was committed to His covenant and purpose for Israel, no matter how much Israel may have tried to thwart God's purposes through their disobedience to him. God's mercy would prevail when it came to the house of Jacob.

Furthermore, not everyone had come under God's condemnation. There were those who had remained faithful to the Lord. Only those who rejected God's Word of judgment would die. They were those who lived under a false pretence before the Lord. They were the people who religiously

---

7. The Syrians and Arameans are the same people; although there is no definitive evidence as to the location of Caphtor, most scholars believe it is the island of Crete; see F. W. Bush, 'Caphtor,' in *The International Standard Bible Encyclopedia*, ed. Geoffrey W. Bromiley, rev. ed. [*ISBE*] (Grand Rapids: Eerdmans, 1979), 1:610-11.

8. The identification of Kir still awaits further evidence; see W. S. Lasor, 'Kir,' in *The International Standard Bible Encyclopedia*, ed. Geoffrey W. Bromiley, rev. ed. [*ISBE*] (Grand Rapids: Eerdmans, 1986), 3:40.

attended the feasts and festivals but were complacent in their worship before the Lord. They were the wealthy who had no regard for those in need. They were the nobles consumed in their pride. They were the king and the religious leaders who used a facade of spirituality for their own selfish ends. They were those who disregarded the opportunities God gave them to repent and be reconciled to Him. They were the people who were arrogant enough to contradict God's Word. All of these people will be removed from the face of the earth.

God's judgment on Israel will be a purifying act of removing the waste from that which will be of use. That which remains will be used for the glory of God by continuing His mission through Israel's being a light to the nations and ultimately God's instrument of salvation. This purifying process was likened to the shaking of grain in a sieve. As a person would shake the sieve the grain would escape, but the sieve would catch that which was undesirable, such as pebbles and dirt, so that it could be thrown away. The phrase, 'no pebble shall fall to the earth' means no person who has rejected the Lord will escape His judgment. The purpose of God's judgment was to remove those who rejected the Lord and save those who had been faithful to Him.

The Lord was committed to His covenant to Israel and the mission to which He had called her. They were to be a kingdom of priests and a holy nation (Exod. 19:6). How could they point the nations to the one true God if they were unfaithful to His law and worshiping him under a false pretence? It not only was an affront to the Lord, but it gave a false testimony of who He was before the other nations. God's people must never forget how our relationship to the Lord encompasses at least three dimensions. First, our faithful obedience and love for God pleases Him. Second, our faithful obedience and love for God will be a blessing to us. Third, our faithful obedience and love for God proclaims to the nations there is only one name by which one may be saved, the name of our Lord Jesus Christ. We must never forget the God who has saved us by His mercy and grace; we must never forget the joy of serving Him; and we must never forget the mission He has given us to go into all the earth and make disciples.

STUDY QUESTIONS

1. How important is it for people to grasp the concept that God is faithful to keep all of His promises, whether they are promises of blessing or judgment?
2. How would the altar become such a shocking place for Israel?
3. Why was it important for the people to understand God's judgment would be inescapable?
4. When does God purpose to do harm to people?
5. How does God demonstrate impartiality in Amos' message?
6. How is God's judgment purifying?
7. How does God deal with an attitude of entitlement?

14

The Lord: The One True Promise Keeper
(Amos 9:11-15)

In July 1991, about 4,200 men attended the first Promise Keepers conference held in an arena. Since its founding in 1990, more than five million men have participated in over one hundred conferences held by Promise Keepers. Many more have listened to their radio, television, and internet broadcasts and have read their printed materials. The organization says, 'Promise Keepers is a Christ-centered organization dedicated to introducing men to Jesus Christ as their Savior and Lord, and then helping them to grow as Christians.' One of the primary ways the organization has attempted to reach these goals has been through what they call their Seven Promises.[1] Since its start, Promise Keepers has encouraged men to adopt these promises as commitments of their own. Randy Phillips, a leader of Promise Keepers, says, 'These promises ... are meant to guide us toward the life of Christ and to transform us within so that we might see transformation in our homes, among our friends, in our churches, and, ultimately, in our nation.'[2]

I have seen the lives of men and their families transformed and truly blessed as a product of the Promise Keepers' minis-

---

1. Information concerning Promise Keepers may be found at their website: http://www.promisekeepers.org/; Internet.
2. Al Janssen and Larry K. Weeden, *Seven Promises of A Promise Keeper* (Colorado Springs: Focus on the Family, 1994), 9.

try. I served with a man who, after sensing God's call at a Promise Keepers conference, left a successful career in order to go to seminary and then into full-time vocational ministry. Even so, I have seen a few men, who were initially enthusiastic and vocal in their commitment to Christ through the Seven Promises, fail in that commitment. I recall one man in particular who committed adultery and caused great damage to at least two families. His failure was no reflection on Promise Keepers. Instead, it was a sign of human depravity. In due course, we all are 'Promise Breakers' at one time or another. There is only one who is a true promise keeper, and that is the Lord God.

Nevertheless, there are times when people may be tempted to believe the Lord is unable or unwilling to keep His promises. One of the times people are often tempted to doubt God's faithfulness to His promises is when they experience His discipline. Like a child who questions a parent's love in the midst of discipline, individuals might think God no longer loves them as they are in the midst of experiencing His correction. God's Word indicates that His discipline upon His children is a sign of His love for them (Heb. 12:6), but just as a child has difficulty understanding this concept with a loving parent, so do many believers when it comes to a loving heavenly Father.

In Amos' day, given the enormity of the devastation God's judgment would bring upon the northern kingdom of Israel, the small remnant of people who had been faithful to the Lord must have wondered if God would keep His promises to Israel. After all, Amos emphatically demonstrated how Israel had broken its covenant with the Lord. Everyone knew that when two parties entered into a covenant and one of the parties broke the covenant, then the other party was no longer obligated to keep his side of the covenant. Therefore, God had every right to abandon Israel. Nevertheless, many years earlier, speaking to Abraham, the Lord said:

> By myself I have sworn, declares the LORD, because you have done this and have not withheld your son, your only son, I will surely bless you, and I will surely multiply your offspring as the stars of heaven and as the sand that is on the seashore. And your offspring shall possess the gate of his enemies, and in your

offspring shall all the nations of the earth be blessed, because you have obeyed my voice (Gen. 22:16-18).

Just as Amos said the Lord swore by Himself that He would bring judgment upon the nation of Israel, the Lord swore by Himself when He established His covenant with Abraham. There could be no stronger language of commitment. Therefore, the Lord was not obligated by Israel; *the Lord was obligated to Himself.* Because of His character, God would keep His promise to Abraham (Gen. 12:1-3; 15:1-21; 17:1-14), which He reaffirmed to Isaac (Gen. 26:24-25) and to Jacob (Gen. 35:9-15). In Numbers 23:19, Balaam recognized this truth concerning the covenant when he said, 'God is not man, that he should lie, or a son of man, that he should change his mind. Has he said, and will he not do it? Or has he spoken, and will he not fulfil it?' Unlike people who are ultimately promise breakers, the Lord will always be faithful as a promise keeper.

Amos' message of impending judgment surely disturbed his audience (7:10). What was to become of those who had remained faithful to the Lord in the midst of such a godless society? Will the Lord abandon His people? Years later, the people in Isaiah's time heard a similar message of God's judgment from Isaiah and must have had the same concerns, but the Lord encouraged them with these words:

> Fear not, for you will not be ashamed; be not confounded, for you will not be disgraced; for you will forget the shame of your youth, and the reproach of your widowhood you will remember no more. For your Maker is your husband, the LORD of hosts is his name; and the Holy One of Israel is your Redeemer, the God of the whole earth he is called. For the LORD has called you like a wife deserted and grieved in spirit, like a wife of youth when she is cast off, says your God. For a brief moment I deserted you, but with great compassion I will gather you. In overflowing anger for a moment I hid my face from you, but with everlasting love I will have compassion on you,' says the LORD, your Redeemer (Isa. 54:4-8).

Likewise, by the time of Amos, the Lord God had made several promises to His people. In order to comfort His people and remove all fear and trepidation, the Lord God of Israel, the one true promise keeper, reaffirmed His commitment to keep those promises to His people in spite of Israel's sin. God's wrath will come to an end, and there will be a day when His people will once again experience His blessing.

God will be faithful to His promise concerning Israel's throne (9:11)
When David was the king over all of Israel, God made an everlasting covenant with him stating that the Lord would establish the throne of David's kingdom forever through his offspring (2 Sam. 7:12-13). Although this covenant was made to David concerning his kingdom, this covenant was for all of Israel. If David were to have a throne that would last over his kingdom forever, then his kingdom must last forever also. The Lord's promise to David was a continuation of His covenant with Israel, revealing how the line of David will eternally rule over the nation. God's promise to David echoed His promise to Abraham. It was David who finally conquered all the land that the Lord had promised to Abraham. Just as with Abraham, God promised to make David's name great and to bless him. Similarly, the Lord promised to maintain a special relationship of blessing with David, as he did with Abraham, through his offspring, especially with the promise of a son who will be his heir. In one of the most noted royal psalms, Psalm 72, this connection between God's purpose for the king and His covenant with Abraham is striking: 'May his name endure forever, his fame continue as long as the sun! May people be blessed in him, all nations call him blessed!' (Ps. 72:17).[3] Therefore, the Davidic king was supposed to embody the blessings and missional purposes of the Lord for the nation of Israel in continuation of the Lord's covenant with Abraham.

Yet with the death of Solomon, the kingdom was rent in two, with Judah in the south ruled by the Davidic line and Israel in the north ruled by various dynasties. So the great kingdom David had ruled became weakened by the split through division, war, suspicion, and competition. The great united kingdom of Israel once ruled by David appeared to be no more.

Nevertheless, the Lord had not forgotten His promise to David. Amos was the first of several classical prophets to

---

3. Christopher J. H. Wright, *Knowing Jesus Through the Old Testament* (Grand Rapids: IVP Academic, 1992), 89-90.

reaffirm God's promise to David.[4] It is interesting to note Amos' use of the term 'booth of David'. One would expect the more common expression of 'house of David'. The word 'booth' means a temporary shelter such as a tent or a lean-to made of branches. Such structures were weak and susceptible to the elements, unlike the royal buildings of that day made of stone and mortar. With the collapse of the united kingdom the once-strong house of David had become so weakened that its condition was like a precarious booth, 'that is, a dilapidated, unstable, precarious state of affairs.'[5] Nonetheless, Amos declared the day will come when the Lord will re-establish the throne of David and his kingdom in all its former glory. Clearly, the apostles in the New Testament recognized Jesus to be the fulfillment of this promised king from the line of David.[6]

God will be faithful to His promise concerning Israel's purpose (9:12)
Just before God established His covenant with Israel at Mount Sinai with the giving of the Ten Commandments, He stated His purpose for Israel. He told the people that they would be His 'treasured possession' and that they would be to Him a 'kingdom of priests' and a 'holy nation' (Exod. 19:4-6). Just as Israel's priests taught the people God's Word and made atonement for Israel, so the Lord's kingdom of priests, Israel, was commissioned to proclaim a knowledge of God to the nations and to make for them a way of atonement to God. As the priests of Israel blessed the nation, so this kingdom of priests was to bless the nations.[7]

What's more, as a holy nation, Israel was distinct and different from all other nations. One aspect of Israel's holiness was its independence of Israel's own action because the Lord

---
4. See Isaiah 1:26; 9:6-7; 11:1-10; 55:3; Jeremiah 23:5-6; 30:9; 33:14-16, 20-26; Ezekiel 34:23-24; 37:24-25; Hosea 3:5; Micah 5:2.
5. Paul, 290.
6. See Matthew 1:1; 2:1-2; 9:27; 12:23; 15:22; 16:16; 20:30-31; 21:5, 9, 15; 22:42-45; 25:31; Mark 10:47-48; 12:35-37; Luke 1:32; 4:41; 19:38-40; John 11:27; 18:33-38; 20:31; Acts 2:30-36; 13:22-23; 17:7; 1 Timothy 1:17; 6:15; Revelation 3:7; 15:3; 17:14; 19:16.
7. For a comprehensive study of Israel's priesthood see T. J. Betts, *Ezekiel the Priest: A Custodian of Tôrâ*, vol. 74 of *Studies in Biblical Literature* (New York: Peter Lang Publishing, 2005), 17-45.

had sanctified the nation to Himself; therefore, they were holy (Lev. 22:15). On the other hand, there was an aspect of Israel's holiness that required action on the part of the people. Since the Lord had made them holy, having distinguished them from all the other nations, they were to be holy. As the Lord was distinct from all the false gods of that day, so Israel was to be distinct from all the other nations of that day. We may see this concern for Israel's distinctiveness in the law. For instance, a separation from the nations was at the heart of laws concerning what was clean and unclean.[8]

> But I have said to you, 'You shall inherit their land, and I will give it to you to possess, a land flowing with milk and honey.' I am the LORD your God, who have separated you from the peoples. You shall therefore separate the clean beast from the unclean, and the unclean bird from the clean. You shall not make yourselves detestable by beast or by bird or by anything with which the ground crawls, which I have set apart for you to hold unclean. You shall be holy to me, for I the LORD am holy and have separated you from the peoples, that you should be mine (Lev. 20:24-26).

We may see another aspect of this concern in the ethical nature of the law. Holiness required a people of integrity, compassion, justice, and righteousness in every aspect of private and public life. In this distinct way, they were supposed to reflect their distinct and holy God before the nations. It was the means by which they, as a redeemed people, were to reflect their Redeemer. That was Israel's purpose as a kingdom of priests. In order to fulfill this purpose, they had to be different from all the other nations.[9]

Amos' oracles against the nations, followed by his message to Israel, demonstrated how Israel had lost its distinctiveness from the other nations. Consequently, Israel would be judged like the other nations. Nevertheless, the Lord refused to forget His promise to Abraham and His descendants to use them as an instrument of blessing to the nations.[10] Nothing could thwart God's purposes for Israel, not even Israel's sin.

---

8. Wright, *Mission of God*, 373-4.
9. Ibid., 375.
10. See Gen. 12:2-3; 15:1-21; 17:1-14; 26:24-25; 35:9-15.

People from every nation that once stood in opposition to Israel and in rebellion to God, as represented by Edom and demonstrated in Amos 1–2, will become the possession, and thus part of Israel under the authority of the coming Son of David who will rule over a restored Israel.[11] Here, Amos foresaw a great reversal. The nations that once stood in opposition to the Lord will one day be called by the name of the Lord. We must not overlook the significance of this statement. The expression 'called by my name' denotes ownership and an intimate relationship. Wright comments:

> To be called by the name of YHWH was the luggage tag of the ark, the dedication plaque on the temple, the map reference of Jerusalem and the lapel badge for every Israelite. It was the defining privilege of only one people on earth—Israel—to be known as 'the nation called by the name of YHWH.' Now, declares the prophet, this identity will be available to people of 'all nations.' How more included could you get?
>
> The nations who stood under God's judgment with Israel in Amos 1–2 now stand under God's blessing with Israel in these closing verses. The very concept of 'Israel' has been stretched to include them in the key designation: 'called by my name.'[12]

Up to this time, of all the nations, only Israel could rightly say she was called by the name of the Lord (Deut. 28:9-10). Here, Amos not only reaffirmed God's intention to use Israel as a blessing to the nations, but he revealed what the result of that blessing would be upon the nations. The council of Jerusalem, mentioned in Acts 15, recognized the ongoing and climactic fulfillment of Amos 9:11-12 with the coming of the Lord Jesus Christ, the Son of David, and the outpouring of God's Spirit upon the Gentiles (Acts 15:16-18).

Today, believers should recognize it has always been in the will of God to use His people as a blessing to the nations. Some give the impression that the Old Testament is all about saving national Israel and the New Testament is about saving Gentiles, the Church. Jonah made a similar false assumption about Israel in his day. It is as if the Great Commission is a new concept. Ultimately, the Lord Jesus Christ fulfilled Israel's purpose of making God known and making a way

---

11. For this understanding of Edom see Garrett, 284; Motyer, 204.
12. Wright, *Mission of God*, 496.

of atonement for the nations. Nevertheless, the numerous Gentiles in the Old Testament who came to faith in the one true God of Israel, such as Rahab, Ruth, and Naaman, to name a few, demonstrate it was always in the heart of God to use the testimony of His people to be a witness to the nations.[13] Their salvation anticipated more to come. It was for this reason the Lord spoke to Israel through His prophet Isaiah:

> All the nations gather together, and the peoples assemble. Who among them can declare this, and show us the former things? Let them bring their witnesses to prove them right, and let them hear and say, It is true. 'You are my witnesses,' declares the LORD, 'and my servant whom I have chosen, that you may know and believe me and understand that I am he. Before me no god was formed, nor shall there be any after me. I, I am the LORD, and besides me there is no savior. I declared and saved and proclaimed, when there was no strange god among you; and you are my witnesses,' declares the LORD, 'and I am God' (Isa. 43:9-12).

God commissioned Israel to be a witness of His salvation to the nations. Amos foresaw a time when the Davidic king will save and possess the nations and include them in a restored and greater kingdom of Israel. Israel will fulfill its purpose of being a kingdom of priests and a holy nation.

God will be faithful to His promise concerning Israel's blessing (9:13-14)

Just before the Israelites entered into the Promised Land, Moses presented blessings and curses to them as consequences of either their faithfulness or unfaithfulness to the Lord. Moses prophesied how Israel would break the covenant with the Lord and how He would bring devastating judgment upon her cities and lands and send the people into exile (Deut. 29:14-29). Over 600 years later, Amos prophesied that this exile was imminent. However, Moses had more to say concerning the exile:

---

13. Along with Wright's *Mission of God*, see Walter C. Kaiser Jr., *Mission in the Old Testament: Israel as a Light to the Nations* (Grand Rapids: Baker Books, 2000) and T. J. Betts, 'The Great Commission in the Old Testament,' in *The Challenge of the Great Commission: Essays on God's Mandate for the Local Church*, ed. Chuck Lawless and Thom S. Rainer (Louisville: Pinnacle Publishers, 2005).

Amos 9:11-15

> And when all these things come upon you, the blessing and the curse, which I have set before you, and you call them to mind among all the nations where the Lord your God has driven you, and return to the Lord your God, you and your children, and obey his voice in all that I command you today, with all your heart and with all your soul, then the Lord your God will restore your fortunes and have compassion on you, and he will gather you again from all the peoples where the Lord your God has scattered you.... And the Lord your God will bring you into the land that your fathers possessed, that you may possess it. And he will make you more prosperous and numerous than your fathers.... The Lord your God will make you abundantly prosperous in all the work of your hand, in the fruit of your womb and in the fruit of your cattle and in the fruit of your ground. For the Lord will again take delight in prospering you, as he took delight in your fathers (Deut. 30:1-3, 5, 9).

Not only did Amos foresee the looming devastation of God's judgment upon Israel, he also saw a time when God's judgment would be complete and be replaced by God's renewed abundant blessing upon Israel. Amos' message attested to how the Lord is faithful to keep His promises of both judgment and blessing.

(1) God will bless the land with fertility (9:13).
The land will be so fertile the reaper will not be able to collect his harvest before it is time for the plowmen to begin breaking the ground for the next season. Normally, the reaping of barley began in April, and the reaping of wheat in May. It was not until after the first rains of October or November that the plowmen began preparing the land for the coming crop. Therefore, there was about a six-month period between the time of reaping and plowing. Amos proclaimed the time will come when God will bless the land with such fertility that there will be no space between the time of reaping one crop and plowing for the next. The reapers will have their hands full trying to get in all of their crops before it is time to begin work toward the next agricultural cycle.

Furthermore, those who tread the grapes with their bare feet (normally during the months of August and September) will not be finished with their work before it is time to sow; those who plant the seeds will need to do their work in November and December.[14] Instead of the normal gap of time between these two activities, those who tread the grapes and those who sow the seed will find themselves working at the same time. Not only will the grapes be harvested in the valleys as normal, but Amos poetically describes a harvest so great in the mountains they 'shall drip sweet wine, and all the hills shall flow with it.' The land will once again overflow with milk and honey.

(2) God will bless the people with satisfaction (9:14)
As the Lord once prospered His people, so He will do it again just as Moses said (Deut. 30:1-10). When the people of Israel return to the Lord, then His blessing of productivity will return to them. Amos described three ways in which Israel will experience restoration and a tremendous reversal of circumstances. First, they will rebuild and inhabit their homes and cities that had been devastated as a result of God's judgment. Second, they will be able to plant vineyards and drink the wine they produce. Third, they will be able to cultivate gardens and enjoy their fruit. God will reverse what He will do when He punishes Israel. No longer will they experience frustration. Earlier in his message, Amos said they will not be able to live in the houses they built nor enjoy the fruit of what they had planted (5:10-11), but there will be a day when they will experience the satisfaction of enjoying the fruits of their labors.

God will be faithful to His promise concerning Israel's inheritance (9:15)
The Lord told Abraham: 'And I will give to you and to your offspring after you the land of your sojournings, all the land of Canaan, for an everlasting possession, and I will be their God' (Gen. 17:8). As Amos concluded his message, he told the people of a time when the Lord will plant in the land of promise those faithful to Him, never to be uprooted again. It is important to recognize what the land symbolized to the people of Israel. Wright says:

---

14. King and Stager, 99-101.

… the land was above all else *God's gift*, given in fulfilment of his promise to Abraham, and received in the course of their redemptive history. It was therefore a huge symbolic, tangible proof to every Israelite that he and his people had a special relationship with God. Deuteronomy links it repeatedly with the assurance of their election in Abraham. They were the LORD's people because they lived in the LORD's land which he had given to them. The individual enjoyed his personal share in the land through the kinship network and his inalienable family inheritance.

Thus, to belong to an Israelite household living in God's land was to experience secure inclusion within the covenant relationship: it was the place of *life* with God. But it also meant to accept the demands of that covenant relationship, so it was also the place of a specific *life-style* before God. To possess the land was to share in the inheritance of all God's people. The land, in short, meant security, inclusion, blessing, corporate sharing and practical responsibility.[15]

Through His prophet Amos, the Lord said He would permanently establish His people in the land when the booth of David is repaired, that is, when the Messiah comes. It is in this Messiah, the Lord Jesus Christ, that we are securely included in a covenant relationship with God. It is in Him we experience *life* and are called to a specific *life-style* before God.[16] It is through faith in the Lord Jesus Christ we enter into the kingdom called by the name of the Lord and experience 'security, inclusion, blessing, corporate sharing and practical responsibility.' Above all else *God's gift* is eternal life in Christ Jesus our Lord (Rom. 6:23).

The conclusion to a message is always important. It is what often leaves the most lasting impression. It is interesting to note that when Amos concluded his message there were two expressions Amos' audience would not forget. The Lord called them 'my people' and He called Himself 'the Lord your God.' There is no greater blessing believers may experience than hearing the Lord say to us, 'You are my people, and I am the Lord your God.'

---

15. Christopher J. H. Wright, *An Eye for An Eye: The Place of Old Testament Ethics Today* (Downers Grove, IL: InterVarsity Press, 1983), 94-5.
16. For an insightful study of 'land' theology in the Scriptures see Elmer A. Martens, *God's Design: A Focus on Old Testament Theology*, 3rd ed. (N. Richland Hills, TX: Bibal Press, 1998), 113-37, 217-36, 299-313, 342-55.

STUDY QUESTIONS

1. To whom was the Lord obligated to keep His covenant?
2. Why was God's covenant with David important to Israel?
3. What was God's purpose for choosing Israel as His covenant people?
4. How does this purpose apply to Amos' message?
5. What does Edom represent in this passage?
6. What did Amos reveal about the result of the nations being blessed?
7. What about the conclusion of the book of Amos should leave a lasting impression?

Conclusion

As one concludes a study of the book of Amos, several key ideas stand out. First, God sometimes uses unlikely people to be His messengers. Amos was an ordinary man in the business of shepherding and growing figs, but the Lord called him to deliver an extraordinary message. Amos was faithful to be obedient to the Lord in spite of the numerous obstacles before him. He apparently lacked any formal training or any human support. Amos went to a people who looked down upon his own people of Judah. Nonetheless, Amos trusted God as he faithfully proclaimed the message God gave him. Amos is an example of a faithful servant of the Lord who interceded for his people and at the same time lovingly proclaimed very difficult messages. Second, all of the nations are under God's rule. The Lord is the God of the nations, and every nation will ultimately answer to God for its actions. This accountability includes Israel. No nation is exempt from answering to God, not even God's chosen people. The nation that had been called to be a kingdom of priests and a holy nation had abandoned its calling. Third, greater blessing calls for greater responsibility. Israel had experienced God's blessing like no other nation. Therefore, God held Israel more responsible for its actions than He did any other people.

Fourth, God expects His people to worship Him with faithful hearts. Israel put on quite a display in its worship, yet its worship lacked sincerity and integrity. The people's worship appeared to be more about them than it did God. It was about what they could get from God rather than what they were offering Him. While they must have been impressed with their religious activities, God was unimpressed. In fact, God rejected such pretentious expressions of worship then as He does today. Fifth, it is impossible to worship the Lord while at the same time mistreating or neglecting others. Israel had become obsessed by materialism. Most people seemed to be consumed with the desire to increase in riches, no matter who it harmed in the process. The wealthy of Israel demonstrated a complete lack of concern for the poor. They took advantage of the needy whenever the opportunity presented itself and even flaunted their ill-gotten gain in their worship. The people who had experienced oppression had become oppressors themselves. Their oppression of the poor led to God's rejection of their so-called acts of worship. Furthermore, it resulted in God's coming judgment.

Sixth, when people are unfaithful to God and lack concern for others, God's judgment is imminent. Such a message was just as unpopular in Amos' day as it is today. Nevertheless, it is true just the same. Just as its agricultural cycle ended each year with the summer fruit, Israel's time had run out. God had demonstrated patience, but Israel had become so hardened to the Lord's message that He would not relent of His judgment. Their ungodliness would result in severe consequences. Seventh, God's message of judgment was also a demonstration of His grace. Amos made the case that Israel certainly deserved God's judgment. Still, God's message of judgment served not only as a warning to Israel but also as one more opportunity for Israel to repent and be restored to the Lord.

Eighth, Amos declared that someday in the future God will restore Israel through the Messiah. In Him, people from all the nations will be brought into the kingdom of God. Even though Israel had disobeyed the Lord and would experience God's judgment and exile, that would not be the end of the story. God's prophet proclaimed the Messiah will usher in a day when Israel will once again experience all of God's blessings and the nation will enjoy its inheritance as the people of God.

Amos may have been an ordinary man, but he preached an extraordinary message.

Subject Index

Abimelech 89, 134
Abraham 89, 134, 182-3, 184, 190-1
accountability, responsibility and 61-4, 193
Adonijah 173
affluence 117-19
agricultural year 154-5
Ahab 27, 33, 68
altar 173-4
Amaziah (king) 10-11
Amaziah (priest) 11, 52, 134, 143-9, 151
American Dream 73-4
Ammon, judgment on 30-3
Amorites 46-7
Amos (prophet)
    background 8-9, 149
    faithfulness 193
    name 7
Amos (book)
    setting 9-15
    source of message 15-16
Aram 12, 23-4, 178
Arameans 116, 178
army, destruction of 54-6
Assyria 39
Assyrians 74-5
atonement 185
authority, ultimate 143-52

Baal 68
Balaam 33, 147, 183
Balak 33, 147
Bashan 71-2
basketball 153-4
Beersheba 89, 168
Ben-ammi 30
Ben-Hadad 23
Bethel 68, 88, 140, 143-4, 168, 171
    children from 151
blessing to the nations 187-8

booths 185
brutality 32
burnt offering 104

Calamities 66, 81
Calneh 116
Canaanites 46-7
Caphtor 178
capitals 174
casemate walls 95
cause and effect 64-6
chiastic structure 86-7
Christ *see* Jesus Christ
Clarke, John 146
commission 150, 187-8
compassion 134, 136, 159
complacency 113-19
consumerism 90
contempt 33-4
covenants 35-6, 179, 182-3, 184, 191
    and judgment 21
    rejection of 36-40
Creator 82, 139-40, 176
curses 77
Cush 177

Damascus 12, 32
    judgment on 23-4
Dan 68, 140, 144, 168
David, kingdom of 184-5
Day of the Lord 99-102, 165
debts 43
deliverance 103
    day of 100-1
deprivation 77-9
destruction 80-1
    pride resulting in 125-6
devastation 156, 182, 189
    pride resulting in 128-9
disciples, mission to make 179

195

discipline of God 64, 77, 182
dishonesty 162-3
disobedience 38
drought 78-9

E
arthquakes 164-5, 174-5
eclipses 165
economic prosperity 13-14
Edom 10, 187
   judgment on 28-30
   Moab and 34
Eglon 33
Egypt
   bondage in 47-8
   locusts 133
Egyptians, as witnesses 67
Ehud 33
El 118
elect 60
Elijah 68
Elisha 31, 144, 151
ephah 162
Esau 28
eternal life 191
evil, hating 94
exile 188-9
Exodus 59-60, 103, 178
exploitation 26

F
aithfulness of God 46
   see also promises of God
false prophets 38-9
false religion 68
famine 16-17, 77-8
Feast of Harvest 103
Feast of Ingathering 103
Feast of Unleavened Bread 103
Feast of Weeks 103
feasts 103-4, 117-19
fertility 189-90
fire 80-1, 135-8
fish-hooks 74-5
fortifications 67-8, 95

G
ath 116-17
Gaza, judgment on 25-6
Gezer Calendar 154-5
gift of God 191
Gilead 23-4, 32
Gilgal 88-9
golden calves 68
Gomorrah 80-1

good, seeking 93
grace of God 52-3, 55, 137, 194
grain offering 104
grapes 189-90
greed 43-4, 157-63

H
amath 116
Hananiah 151
Hannah 50
hardening of heart 83
harm 175-6
harp 105
hatred 28-30
Hazael 23-4, 81
Hell 102
Hezekiah 39, 118
Hitler, Adolf 146
holiness 186
Holmes, Obadiah 146
holy nation 185-6
hope 69
human trafficking 163
hypocrisy 45-6

I
dolatry 109-10
immorality 45
infliction 79-80
inheritance, land as 49, 190-1
injustice 91
integrity 161-3
intercession 134-6
invulnerability 114-15
Iran 146
Isaac 89, 140, 183
Israel
   blessing of 188-90
   as blessing to the nations 187-8
   as chosen people 177
   death of 86-92, 96
   distinctiveness 186
   establishment as people 59
   God of 82
   inheritance 49, 190-1, 194
   judgment on
     see judgment on Israel
   purpose 185-8
   remnant of 69, 178
   throne 184-5

J
acob 28, 88, 89, 183
Jehoash 10-11, 23
Jehoram 33

Subject Index

Jehu 144
Jeremiah 151
Jeroboam I 68, 144, 171
Jeroboam II 23, 116-17, 141-2, 144-5
    army under 54
    house of 140, 141-2, 151
Jerusalem
    council of 187
    destruction 39
Jesus Christ
    authority of 150-1
    as king from line of David 185
    as Messiah 191
    second coming of 172
Jezebel 27, 73
Joab 173
John the Baptist 101
Jonah 187
Joram 144
Jordan Rift Valley 164
Joseph 132
Joshua 46, 89
Josiah 171-2
Jotham 39
Judah, judgment on 35-40
Judas Maccabees 33
Judge, the Lord as 82
judgment on Israel 41-56, 131-42, 154-7, 171-9, 194
    certainty of 171-6
    impartiality of 177-9
    as inescapable 174-5
    as purposeful 175-6
    reasons for 157-63
    as scornful 173-4
    sovereignty of 176-7
judgment on neighbors 19-40
justice 93

K

Karnaim 127
Khomeini, Ayatollah 146
kindness
    failure to show 52-3
    of God 46-51
king, authority 143-6, 148
kingdom of priests 185-6
kinnor 105
Kir 178
Kiyyun 108-9
Korah 151

L

Laments 86, 166
Law *see tôrâ*

laziness 158
Leming, Josiah 99
lions 65
Lo-debar 127
locusts 79, 132-5
Lot 30-1, 33
lyre 105

M

Materialism 163, 194
Menahem 31-2
mercy of God 66, 137
Mesha 33
Messiah 191, 194
Micah 93
military superiority 12-13
military victories 100
mission 179
Moab
    Edom and 34
    judgment on 33-5
morality, as personal 139
Moses, intercessory prayer 134
music 105-6

N

Naboth 73
name of the Lord 187
national disunity 9-12
nations, accountability to God 183
Nazirites 50-1
nebel 105
Nebuchadnezzar 33, 35, 39
neighbor, loving 22
new moon festival 160
Nile River, flooding 164-5

O

Oaths 124, 164
Obadiah 28
obedience 16
opposition 80, 148-9, 151-2
    to gospel 145-6
oppression 42-5, 52, 158, 194
    end to 69
    opposition of God to 54
Orion 94
orphans 157-8
ownership 187

P

Passing by 156
Passover 103
patience of God 21-2
peace offering 104-5

Subject Index

Pentecost ... 103
Pharaoh ... 132
Philistines ... 25-6, 67, 116-17, 178
Phillips, Randy ... 181
Phoenicians ... 27
plague ... 80
Pleiades ... 94
plowing ... 189
plumb line ... 138-42, 147
plummet ... 139
poor, treatment of ... 44-6, 157-60
positive thinking ... 91
pride ... 44-5, 115, 121-9
  and death ... 125
  and delusional thinking ... 127-8
  and destruction ... 125-6
  and devastation ... 128-9
  as idolatry ... 123
  and poor judgment ... 126-7
  Scripture on ... 122-3
privileges ... 57-61
processions ... 110
profanity ... 107
Promise Keepers ... 181-2
Promised Land, entrance into ... 89
promises of God ... 182-91
  concerning Israel's blessing ... 188-90
  concerning Israel's inheritance 190-1
  concerning Israel's purpose ... 185-8
  concerning Israel's throne ... 184-5
prophets
  authority ... 149-50
  opposition to ... 51-2
  role ... 49-50
purifying process ... 179

Qayic ... 155
qēc ... 155

Rabbah ... 32
reaping ... 189
reconciliation, call of ... 96
rejection, of God by people ... 87-92
relenting of God ... 136-8
religious activity ... 15, 75-6, 160
  substitution for devotion to God ... 88-90, 92-3
religious establishment, authority ... 146-9
repentance, as too late ... 82-3
repetition ... 157
residences ... 69
responsibility ... 16, 57
  and accountability ... 61-4, 193

privilege of ... 57-61
restoration ... 190, 194
Retribution Principle ... 13
revelation ... 82, 150
rhetoric, substitution for reality ... 90-1
rocky terrain ... 126

Sabbath ... 161
sacred places ... 88-90, 140, 143-4, 171-2
sacrifices ... 104-5, 108
salvation, message of ... 137-8
Samson ... 50
Samuel ... 50, 134
sanctuary ... 173
Sardis ... 87
Saul ... 25, 28, 33, 89
seasons ... 154-5
  control of ... 94
second coming of Christ ... 172
security, sources of ... 67-9
seeking, of God ... 92-4
seer ... 146
self-absorption ... 71-4
self-centeredness ... 71-83
self-deception ... 75-7
self-delusion ... 77
self-gratification ... 119
self-importance ... 115
self-reliance ... 81-3
Sennacherib ... 39, 118
separation ... 186
sexual violence ... 29
shekel ... 162
shepherds ... 68
shrines *see* sacred places
Sikkuth ... 108
sinning
  against God ... 63-4
  against kinsmen ... 62
  against nations ... 62-3
  against selves ... 61-2
sins, and judgment ... 20
siroccos ... 79
slavery ... 163
  deliverance from ... 47-8
Sodom ... 80-1, 134
sovereignty of God ... 21, 94-6, 176
spiritual leadership ... 49-50
Stirling Bridge ... 114
strength ... 54
summer fruit ... 153-5
sun, eclipse of ... 165
superiority, sense of ... 115-17
swiftness ... 54

Subject Index

sycamore trees 149
Syrians 81

Ten Commandments 62
threshing 23-4
Tiglath-Pileser III 31
tôrâ, rejection of 36, 39
traps 65-6
Twain, Mark 96
Tyre, judgment on 26-8

Unfaithfulness, response of
God to 77-81
Uzziah 9-13, 39, 117

Visions 131-42
vocation 150

Walking 65
Wallace, William 114
watchmen 66
water 106
widows 157-8
wilderness, provision in 49
Williams, Roger 146
Word of God
  blessing of 58-9
  famine of 166-7
  importance 37
  latching on to 166-9
worms 79
worship
  corporate 105-6, 160-1
  true 76-7, 140-1, 193-4

Zechariah 144

Scripture Index

Genesis
2:2 136
6:6 136
12:1-3 .... 16, 36, 183
12:2-3 186
12:7 49
12:10 77
15:1-21 .... 183, 186
15:5 59
15:18-21 49
17:1-14 .... 183, 186
17:8 .... 49, 190
18:19 60
18:23-33 134
18:25 82
19:30-38 .... 30, 33
20:7 134
21:22 89
21:31-32 89
22:16-18 183
22:17 59
26:4 49
26:24 89
26:24-25 .... 183, 186
28:4 49
28:13-14 49
28:15 88
31:39 68
35:9-15 .... 183, 186
35:10-12 88
35:12 49
41:25 132
41:32 132
44:21 175
46:2-4 89
48:22 46
50:24 49

Exodus
1:9-14 48
2:23 48
10:12 133

12:1-28 103
12:12 88
12:22-23 156
12:23 88
13:6-10 103
13:21-22 49
15:7 136
16:13-16 49
17:6 49
19:4-6 185
19:4-8 36
19:5 .... 35, 48
19:6 179
20:8-10 161
21:2-11 43
21:13-14 .... 68, 173
21:20-21 159
21:26-27 159
21:32 48
22:12-13 68
22:22-24 158
22:26 46
23:10-11 159
23:14-17 103
23:20-23 47
31:18 136
32:13 59
33 140
33:12 60
33:17 60
34:6-7 134
34:22 103
34:22-23 103
34:25 103
40:21 49

Leviticus
1–5 75
3:11 104
3:16 104
7:13-15 75
7:16 76

16:18 68
19:18 44
19:35-36 162
20:24-26 186
22:15 186
23:16 103
23:16-21 103
23:33-43 103
23:36 104
25 159
25:23 159
25:25 159
25:35 159
25:39 159
25:42-43 163
25:46 163
25:47 159
25:53 163
25:55 163
26:25 80

Numbers
2:2 49
6:1-20 50
10:33 49
11:4 101
11:34 101
13:28 46
13:33 47
14:11-14 134
14:12 80
14:31-32 134
16:1-40 151
22–25 33
23:19 183
26:52-56 159
28:26 103
29:35 104

Deuteronomy
1:27 47
1:28 46

200

Scripture Index

2:10 46
2:19 31
2:21 46
4:5-6 45
4:37 60
5:21 101
6:5 .... 44, 64
6:10-12 124
6:13 64
7:6 48
9:2 46
9:24 60
10:12 64
10:12-13 61
10:20 64
10:22 59
11:1 64
11:13 64
11:24 82
14:2 48
14:28-29 .... 75, 159
15:1-18 159
15:12-18 .... 43, 159
16:8 104
16:13-15 103
23:7 28
24:6 159
24:10-13 159
24:14 159
24:17-22 158
24:18-22 159
24:22 159
25:5-10 159
25:13-16 162
26:5 59
26:6-7 48
26:12-13 160
26:18 48
26:19 60
27–28 .... 64, 77
28:9-10 187
28:21 80
28:22 79
28:23 79
28:23-24 78
28:25 80
28:28-29 102
28:38 79
28:47-48 77
28:63 136
29:14-29 188
30:1-3 189
30:1-10 190
30:5 189
30:9 189

30:15-20 16
32:14 72
32:46-47 167
33:2-4 58
33:10 104
33:29 82

Joshua
4:20 89
5:2-12 89
5:13-15 89
6:2 89
9:6 89
10:6-43 89
14:6 89
14:12 46
14:15 46
15:14 46
24:5-8 49
24:15 46

Judges
3:12-14 .... 31, 32
3:12-30 33
5:30 29
6:10 46
10:6–11:33 31
13:3-5 50
13:7 51

1 Samuel
1:11 50
5–6 80
7:5-13 134
7:9 104
11:1-11 31
11:14-15 89
12:18-23 134
14:47 .... 28, 33
16:7 107
20:5 160
22:5 146

2 Samuel
7:12-13 184
8:2 33
8:12 31
8:13-14 28
10:1-14 31
12:1-13 42
12:31 31
21:2 46
24:11 146
24:15 80

1 Kings
1:50 68
1:50-51 173
2:28 68
2:28-29 173
4:21 49
5:12 27
9:13 27
11:14-16 32
12:26-33 144
12:26–13:6 171
12:28-33 68
13:1-2 68
13:4 52
15:27 25
16:15-18 25
16:31 27
18:4 52
19:2 52
19:10 52
21 73
22:26-27 52

2 Kings
1:1 33
2:23-24 151
3:1-27 33
3:4 8
4:23 160
6:31 52
7:1-20 151
8:12 31
8:20-22 28
9–10 144
9:30-37 73
10:20 104
10:32-33 23
12:17-18 23
12:20 144
13:25 23
14:13-14 11
14:19 144
14:23 177
14:23-29 12
14:24 177
14:25-26 117
14:25-27 .... 23, 31
14:28 117
14:29 144
15:8-10 144
15:16 32
17:13 146
24:1-3 .... 31, 32

2 Chronicles
11:5-12 8
15:2 96
17:2 8
17:11 25
20:1-30 31
21:9 146
21:16-17 25
25:5-13 10
25:13 10
25:21-24 11
26:6-7 117
26:6-15 12
26:10 8
26:16-23 39
27:5 31
29:25 146

Nehemiah
4:1-3 31
8:18 104
9:20-21 49

Esther
2:12 118

Job
9:8 82
31:16-23 44

Psalms
10:4 126
19:7 167
22:12 72
24:3-4 ....76, 141
31:23 122
47 124
47:8 136
51 108
51:16-17 108
51:19 ....104, 108
66:18 ....76, 141
72 184
72:17 184
77:18 165
78:5 58
83 27
91:13 82
95:7-8 83
100:3 128
106:40 136
119 38
119:9-11 37
124:6-8 65
136 100
150 105

Proverbs
2:10 127
6:13 127
11:2 122
12:11 158
13:4 101
14:23 158
15:25 122
16:18 ....105, 122
16:32 30
18:12 123
20:13 158
21:17 ....118, 158
21:26 101
22:22 44
22:24-25 30
23:3 101
23:6 101
24:1 101
26:12 126
29:23 123
30:21 165

Ecclesiastes
9:7-8 118

Song of Solomon
1:3 118
4 72
7 72

Isaiah
1 17
1:13 104
1:13-14 160
1:26 185
2:13 72
5:7-25 17
6:3 87
7:18 136
9:6-7 185
11:1-10 185
13:11 123
24:5 140
24:19-20 165
26:15 31
28:1 14
29:10 146
30:10 ....52, 146
34:3 80
42:20 166
43:8-13 36
43:9-12 188
44:14 46
45:7 66

Scripture Index
47:11 175
54:4-8 183
55:3 185
63:3 82

Jeremiah
1:5 60
2:30 52
6:26 166
11:21 52
18:7-8 50
18:18 52
20:10 52
23:5-6 185
24:6 175
26:23 52
28:1-17 151
30:9 185
33:14-16 185
33:20-26 185
34:18 140
39:12 175
40:4 175
49:16 123
50:19 72

Lamentations
1:15 82

Ezekiel
5:5-9 40
13:4-5 134
14:19 80
21:17 136
22:30 134
24:16-24 156
27:5-6 46
27:6 72
34:23-24 185
37:24-25 185
39:18 72
46:1 160
46:3 160

Hosea
2:13 160
3:5 185
8:6 168
10:8 168
12:8 14
13:5 60
13:16 32

Joel
1:14 104
2:10 165

Scripture Index

2:15 104
2:20 80
3:4-8 27

Amos
1–2 187
1:1 .... 8, 146, 165, 174
1:1-2 .... 7, 54
1:2 65
1:3 32
1:3-5 .... 22, 23
1:3–2:3 100
1:3–2:5 19
1:6 163
1:6-8 .... 22, 25
1:9 163
1:9-10 .... 22, 26
1:11-12 .... 22, 28
1:13-15 .... 22, 30
2:1-3 .... 23, 33
2:4-5 .... 23, 35
2:6 163
2:6-8 42
2:6-16 41
2:9-11 46
2:10 108
2:12 .... 51, 147
2:13 52
2:14-16 .... 54, 87
3:1 58
3:1-2 58
3:1-2a 58
3:1-15 57
3:3 65
3:3-6 64
3:4 65
3:5 65
3:7 82
3:7-8 66
3:8 65
3:9-10 67
3:11-12 67
3:11-15 67
3:13-14 68
3:15 .... 14, 69
4:1 58
4:1-3 71
4:1-13 71
4:2 .... 74, 164
4:2-3 145
4:3 75
4:4-5 75
4:6-8 77
4:6-11 77
4:6-13 14

4:9 132
4:9-10a 79
4:10 87
4:10b 80
4:11 80
4:12 174
4:12-13 81
5:1 58
5:1-3 87
5:1-17 .... 85, 86
5:4-6 .... 87, 92
5:5 .... 87, 145, 168
5:7 .... 87, 139
5:8-9 .... 87, 94
5:10-11 190
5:10-13 87
5:14 90
5:14-15 .... 87, 92
5:15 93
5:16-17 87
5:18 .... 100, 165
5:18-20 .... 99, 100
5:18-27 99
5:19 101
5:20 .... 102, 165
5:21 104
5:21-24 103
5:21-25 103
5:21-27 99
5:23 105
5:24 .... 106, 139
5:25 108
5:26-27 .... 108, 145
6:1-2 114
6:1-3 115
6:1-7 .... 113, 114
6:1-14 99
6:4-6 14
6:4-7 117
6:7 145
6:8 164
6:8-14 .... 121, 124
6:9-10 125
6:11 125
6:12 .... 126, 139
6:13 54
6:14 128
7 143
7:1-3 .... 131, 132
7:1-9 131
7:3 135
7:4-6 .... 131, 135
7:7-9 .... 131, 138
7:8 140

7:9 141
7:10 .... 143, 183
7:10-13 11
7:10-17 .... 8, 143
7:11 .... 87, 151
7:12-13 .... 52, 134
7:14 8
7:15 150
8 154
8:1-3 .... 131, 154, 157
8:1-14 153
8:4 157
8:4-6 157
8:5 .... 160, 161
8:6 .... 162, 163
8:7-10 .... 163, 174
8:11-14 .... 17, 166
9:1 174
9:1-4 .... 131, 171
9:1-4a 174
9:1-10 171
9:4 .... 145, 178
9:4b 175
9:5-6 176
9:5a 176
9:5b 176
9:5c 176
9:6a 176
9:6b 176
9:6c 176
9:7-10 177
9:8 178
9:10 100
9:11 184
9:11-12 187
9:11-15 181
9:12 185
9:13 189
9:13-14 188
9:14 190
9:15 190

Micah
1:3-4 82
3:7 146
5:2 185
6:8 93
7:14 72

Habakkuk
3:6 165

Zephaniah
2:8-11 31

Scripture Index

Zechariah
11:1-2 46
11:2 72
12:10 166
14:4 165

Malachi
3:17 48

Matthew
1:1 185
2:1-2 185
3:9-10 101
5:11 145
6:25-34 49
6:33 .... 90, 150
7:15-23 93
7:15-27 39
7:21-27 111
9:27 185
12:23 185
13:41-42 138
15:22 185
16:16 185
18:23-34 53
20:30-31 185
21:5 185
21:9 185
21:15 185
22:37-40 44
22:42-45 185
23:37-38 134
25:31 185
25:31-46 63
28:18 150
28:20 49

Mark
7:6-7 169
7:21-23 38
10:47-48 185
12:35-37 185

Luke
1:32 185
4:41 185
12:47-48 37
12:48b 64
13:6-9 83
14:11 123
18:13 83
19:38-40 185

John
1:1-14 59
3:16-17 138

5:22-27 82
8:31 37
8:32 37
8:34-36 37
8:39 55
9:1-3 13
10:1 141
11:27 185
14:6 141
14:17 49
15:5 .... 8, 127
18:33-38 185
20:31 185

Acts
2:30-36 185
5:28-29 152
13:22-23 185
15 187
15:16-18 187
17:7 185

Romans
1:18-32 21
2:4-6 14
2:14-15 21
3:2 58
3:25 137
4:13 49
4:17 92
6:23 191
8:11 49
8:16-17 49
8:34 136
9:7 55
13:12-14 45

1 Corinthians
3:16 49
6:19 49
10:12 115
15:55-57 47

2 Corinthians
5:10 82
5:17 92
10:5 128

Galatians
3:29 49
6:2 44
6:7-9 64
6:7-10 44

Ephesians
1:4 137
2:8-9 55

2:10 56
3:10–4:3 56
4:15 67
4:31 30
5:8-20 45

Philippians
4:8-9 141
4:13 8

Colossians
1:13-14 59

1 Thessalonians
2:12 59

1 Timothy
1:17 185
6:15 185

2 Timothy
1:13 37
1:14 .... 37, 49
2:1 37
2:2 37
3:5 102
3:16-17 50
4:1-5 39
4:18 59

Titus
3:3-7 49

Hebrews
1:1 58
1:2 59
1:8 59
3:7-13 168
4:7 83
5:11–6:8 22
10:26 22
12:6 182
12:15 30
12:16-17 22
12:28 59
13:5 49
13:8 81

James
1:22-25 37
2:5 59
2:13 66
4:6 122
5:16 135

Scripture Index

1 Peter
1:19 137
1:20 137
4:12 149
4:17 174

2 Peter
1:11 59
3:1-9 172
3:9 .... 66, 137

1 John
1:9 137

3 John
11 93

Revelation
3:1 87
3:7 185
13:8 137
15:3 185
17:14 185
19:16 185

Focus on the Bible Commentary Series

Deuteronomy: The Commands of a Covenant God – Allan Harman
ISBN 978-1-84550-268-3
Joshua: No Falling Words – Dale Ralph Davis
ISBN 978-1-84550-137-2
Judges: Such a Great Salvation – Dale Ralph Davis
ISBN 978-1-84550-138-9
Ruth & Esther: God Behind the Seen – A. Boyd Luter/Barry C. Davis
ISBN 978-1-85792-805-9
1 Samuel: Looking on the Heart – Dale Ralph Davis
ISBN 978-1-85792-516-6
2 Samuel: Out of Every Adversity – Dale Ralph Davis
ISBN 978-1-84550-270-6
1 Kings The Wisdom and the Folly – Dale Ralph Davis
ISBN 978-1-84550-251-5
2 Kings: The Power and the Glory – Dale Ralph Davis
ISBN 978-1-84550-096-2
1 Chronicles: God's Faithfulness to the People of Judah – Cyril J. Barber
ISBN 978-1-85792-935-5
2 Chronicles: God's Blessing of His Faithful People – Cyril J. Barber
ISBN 978-1-85792-936-2
Psalms 1-89: The Lord Saves – Eric Lane
ISBN 978-1-84550-180-8
Psalms 90-150: The Lord Reigns – Eric Lane
ISBN 978-1-84550-202-7
Proverbs: Everyday Wisdom for Everyone – Eric Lane
ISBN 978-1-84550-267-6
Song of Songs – Richard Brooks
ISBN 978-1-85792-486-2
Isaiah: A Covenant to be Kept for the Sake of the Church – Allan Harman
ISBN 978-1-84550-053-5
Daniel: A Tale of Two Cities – Robert Fyall
ISBN 978-1-84550-194-5
Hosea – Michael Eaton
ISBN 978-1-85792-277-6

FOCUS ON THE BIBLE COMMENTARY SERIES

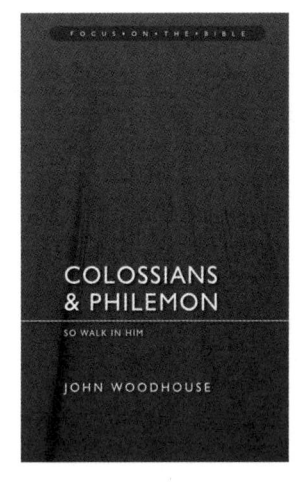

Jonah, Michah, Nahum, Nahum & Zephaniah – John L. Mackay
ISBN 978-1-85792-392-6
Haggai, Zechariah & Malachi: God's Restored People – John L. Mackay
ISBN 978-1-85792-067-3
Matthew: Can Anything Good Come Out of Nazareth – Charles Price
ISBN 978-1-85792-285-1
Mark: Good News from Jerusalem – Geoffrey Grogan
ISBN 978-1-85792-905-8
Acts: Witnesses to Him – Bruce Milne
ISBN 978-1-84550-507-3
Romans: The Revelation of God's Righteousness – Paul Barnett
ISBN 978-1-84550-269-0
1 Corinthians: Holiness and Hope of a Rescued People – Paul Barnett
ISBN 978-1-84550-721-3
2 Corinthians: The Glories & Responsibilities of Christian Service – Geoffrey Grogan
ISBN 978-1-84550-252-2
Galatians: God's Proclamation of Liberty – Joseph A. Pipa Jr.
ISBN 978-1-84550-558-5
Ephesians: Encouragement and Joy in Christ – Paul Gardner
ISBN 978-1-84550-264-5
Colossians & Philemon: So Walk in Him – John Woodhouse
ISBN 978-1-84550-632-2
1 & 2 Thessalonians: Triumphs and Trials of a Consecrated Church – Richard Mayhue
ISBN 978-1-85792-452-7
James: Wisdom for the Community – Christopher Morgan/Dale Ellenburg
ISBN 978-1-84550-335-2
1 Peter – Derek Cleave
ISBN 978-1-85792-337-7
2 Peter & Jude – Paul Gardner
ISBN 978-1-85792-338-4
1, 2 & 3 John – Michael Eaton
ISBN 978-1-85792-152-6
Revelation: The Compassion and Protection of Christ – Paul Gardner
ISBN 978-1-85792-329-2

Christian Focus Publications

publishes books for all ages
Our mission statement –

STAYING FAITHFUL
In dependence upon God we seek to impact the world through literature faithful to His infallible Word, the Bible. Our aim is to ensure that the LORD Jesus Christ is presented as the only hope to obtain forgiveness of sin, live a useful life and look forward to heaven with Him.

REACHING OUT
Christ's last command requires us to reach out to our world with His gospel. We seek to help fulfil that by publishing books that point people towards Jesus and help them develop a Christ-like maturity. We aim to equip all levels of readers for life, work, ministry and mission.

Books in our adult range are published in three imprints.

Christian Focus contains popular works including biographies, commentaries, basic doctrine and Christian living. Our children's books are also published in this imprint.

Mentor focuses on books written at a level suitable for Bible College and seminary students, pastors, and other serious readers. The imprint includes commentaries, doctrinal studies, examination of current issues and church history.

Christian Heritage contains classic writings from the past.

Christian Focus Publications, Ltd
Geanies House, Fearn, Ross-shire,
IV20 1TW, Scotland, United Kingdom
info@christianfocus.com

www.christianfocus.com